German Doll Marks
&
Identification Book

by Jürgen & Marianne Cieslik

Hobby House Press™

Published by   Cumberland, Maryland 21502

Additional Copies Available @ $6.95 plus $1.25 postage
From
Hobby House Press, Inc.
900 Frederick Street
Cumberland, MD 21502

Additional Copies Available @ $7.95 plus $1.25 postage
from
Hobby House Press, Inc.
Cumberland, MD 21502

ISBN: 0-87588-273-0

Table of Contents

Number series 171, socket head, sleep eyes, open mouth, ball-jointed body. *Ilka Zimmer Collection.*

made in
a 1/3 Germany.
171

Foreword

Because of the great variety of molds and models which have been produced in the long history of the German doll industry, it is risky to make systematic tables of the various products. Every porcelain factory had its own numbering system, which seldom consisted of sequentially numbered series. Often the production was brought together in groups of numbers which would indicate an internal numbering system. Other systems seem to have a coherent order of numbers. Only an intensive study shows that the apparent missing numbers have nothing to do with the doll production of a porcelain factory.

Most of the porcelain factories also produced nick-nacks — half-dolls, vases or religious figures, which were included in the number series. There were only a few factories which made both the doll heads and the bodies. Specialization of work was significant for the German doll industry. In other words, some porcelain factories only made doll heads, which they sold to various doll factories. The larger doll factories designed their own models which were produced to their order by the porcelain factories. The marks on these heads mostly refer to the doll factory — seldom to the porcelain factory. This "Identification Book" is an attempt to determine which porcelain factories made the heads, and to identify the doll manufacturer by a description of the doll itself. Often it is not easy to identify the maker of a doll. While the heads were made in the various porcelain factories, it was the doll makers who assembled the parts — heads, bodies, arms and legs — to make the whole doll. This system caused a great incentive for the porcelain factories to put many models on the market. Great quantities were ordered by the doll makers and assembled. Therefor these doll heads bear the mold numbers of the porcelain factories, and there is no indication as to who actually made the complete doll.

There are only a few opportunities to identify the doll factory. Important clues are the "DRP" and "DRGM" numbers, as well as the producer's name or mark stamped on the doll bodies. Dolls having the original labels with the name of the model or line are invaluable documentation as to the actual doll factory. Very helpful, also, are the stickers or labels on boxes and containers. Unfortunately, these clues are often lost over the years and can only be found on completely original dolls. These are often the only possibility of identifying the maker and exact date of manufacture.

The "Identification Book" is the first addenda to the *German Doll Encyclopedia, 1800-1939,* by Jürgen & Marianne Cieslik. It is arranged so that every doll enthusiast, collector or dealer, can work with it without having to refer to the large "German Doll Encyclopedia" picture-volume. However, for indepth information about German doll production and doll and porcelain factories, the reader must refer to the "Encyclopedia." The "Identification Book" also contains references to illustrations which can be found in the "Encyclopedia."

Trademarks and labels which have been registered, or have been found on dolls, are presentd in a special section. This is the first time there has been an attempt to arrange the various marks and labels into well defined groups.

For the most part, the system we have used relies on number series. Two-figure numbers mostly refer to sizes. For example, the common dolly-face dolls from about 1902 which were produced for Kämmer & Reinhardt by Simon & Halbig. The same is typical for other manufacturers of the late character dolls. Only a few porcelain factories, such as Gebr. Kuhnlenz, Theodor Recknagel, Heinrich Handwerck and Max Rader, used a two-figure number series. Since there was no agreement between the porcelain and doll factories on a number series, every porcelain factory developed their own system. Because of this there are many dolls which have the same mold number, but were made by different factories; they were also made at different times. In order to make a temporal distinction and avoid disparities in terms there was the typical dolly-face with glass eyes and open or closed mouth made until about 1910, and since 1909 the term "character doll" came into use. The date only gives an indication of when a doll was made, but it does not indicate how long it was produced. Some molds were used for more than 40 years with only minor alterations — for example the Armand Marseille 390. If a doll does not correspond exactly with the brief description given in this book, it should be remembered that many models of doll heads were put on the market in several variations. The same model could have been made with painted or glass eyes, open or closed mouths, bald-headed or cut-out for a wig; or as a socket head or shoulder head in all sizes.

If the date given refers to a "GM" (Geschmacksmuster = design patent), it is reliable as far as the beginning of the production of the doll is concerned. (See *German Doll Encyclopedia, 1800-1939*). Dolls which were registered as a "GM" often carry in addition the marking "dep" (deponiert).

Important: This "Identification Book" only deals with doll heads — not small all-bisque dolls or half-dolls (there are few exceptions). There are no references to the Rheinische Gummi-und Celluloidfabrik because the authors are planning a special publication on this firm. There are no other celluloid factories covered, because they seldom used a number series to mark their products. The "Identification Book" does not claim to include all doll heads which have been made. It would be presumptuous to list all models and types produced by the German doll industry. We tried hard to make use of all the information we received from people all over the world for this volume. It is our hope to complete and improve this documentation over the coming years. We will be very grateful for every bit of information we receive from all enthusiasts, collectors and dealers. This includes any descriptions of special doll types, as well as unusual models which have not been listed in this book. It is our intention to publish this book in the future as a picture volume. If there is a reference to an illustration the doll can be found in the "Encyclopedia," and the illustration is on file in our archives. We would be very grateful for any help given to us to complete our documentation, especially by providing photographs of your dolls. We would like to thank all of our friends in advance.

We have chosen a rather unusual way to produce this book. All details come from a data bank which is stored in our computer. This is the only way to assemble a master file of all the information we have gathered about old dolls and their makers. Therefor we decided to print the text directly from the output of the computer. This way of presenting facts and dates adds to their authenticity. Any additional corrections and additions to the data about the German doll industry are thereby much easier and quicker to record and document.

Jülich, Germany,
Spring 1986   JÜRGEN & MARIANNE CIESLIK

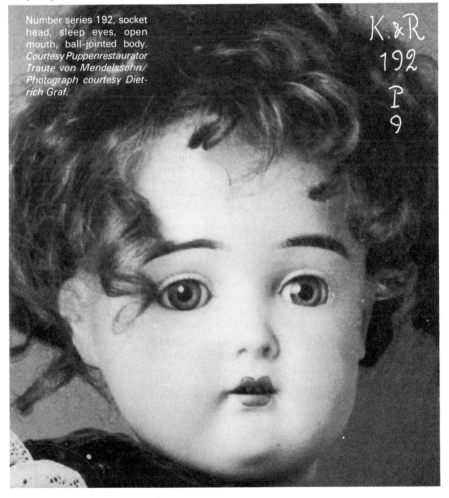

Number series 192, socket head, sleep eyes, open mouth, ball-jointed body. *Courtesy Puppenrestaurator Traute von Mendelssohn/ Photograph courtesy Dietrich Graf.*

1 Bayer. Celluloid-warenfabrik formerly Albert Wacker. **2** Iris Beaumont 1922. **3** Carl Bergner. **4** Rolf Berlich 1923. **5** Bing Künstlerpuppen 1925. **6** Geo. Borgfeldt & Co 1903. **7** Wilhelm Buschow 1929. **8** Robert Carl. **9** Catterfelder Puppenfabrik. **10** E. Dehler. **11** Theodor Degenring. **12** Creidlitz AG. **13** Josef Deuerlein 1907. **14 & 15** Julius Dorst. **16 & 17** Cuno & Otto Dressel. **18** Gebr. Eckardt after 1930.

1

2

3

4

5

6

7

8

9

10

11

12

13

14

15

16

17

18

Circles

19 Gebr. Eckardt for "SECO" Strauss-Eckardt Co. NY. **20** Eisenmann & Co. 1895. **21** J. G. Escher & Sohn 1921. **22** Carl Feiler & Co. 1903. **23 & 24** Fischer, Naumann & Co. **25** Fleischmann & Craemer. **26** Florig & Otto 1920. **27** Gustav Förster. **28 & 29** Friedrichsrodaer Puppenfabrik. **30** Otto Gans 1930. **31** Carl Geyer & Co. 1895. **32** Georg Gebert. **33** Walter Goebel 1928. **34** Arthur Gotthelf 1922. **35 & 36** Ernst Grossmann.

9

37 Erich Hachmeister 1908. 38 Adolf Heller 1925. 39 Henze & Steinhäuser 1925. 40 Hertwig & Co. 1925. 41 Gebr. Heubach. 42 Adolf Hülss 1925. 43 Walter Jügelt 1923. 44 J.D. Kestner jr. 1888. 45 Rose O'Neill. 46 Charlotte N. Kirchhoff 1925. 47 Kley & Hahn 1903. 48 Kley & Hahn 1904. 49 Kley & Hahn 1916. 50 Erich Kloetzer. 51 Koenig & Wernicke 1914. 52 & 53 Koenig & Wernicke. 54 Kohl & Wengenroth.

55 Käthe Kruse 1912. **56** Gebr. Kühnlenz AG. **57** Adolf Landsberger 1908. **58** H. J. Leven. **59** Ernst Liebermann. **60** Heinrich Liebermann 1927. **61** Loeffler & Dill. **62** Sonneberger Porzellanfabrik former. A. Marseille, at the end of the 1940's. **63** Mittelland-Gummiwerke 1927. **64** Moritz Pappe 1907. **65** Emil Pfeiffer. **66** Dora Petzold 1920. **67** Phoenix Gummipuppen. **68 & 69** Porzellanfabrik Mengersgereuth. **70** Theodor Recknagel. **71** Curt F. Reinhardt 1921. **72** Julius Rempel.

55

56

57

58

59

60

61

62

63

64

65

66

67

68

69

70

71

72

73 Scheyer & Co. 1920. **74** Franz Schmidt & Co. 1893. **75** Franz Schmidt & Co. C. 1900. **76** Franz Schmidt & Co. 1907. **77** Paul Schmidt 1923. **78** Robert Schneider Coburg 1924. **79 & 80** Arthur Schoenau. **81** Emil Schwenk. **82** Sigismund Schwerin Succes. 1923. **83** Seyfarth & Reinhardt 1923. **84** Margarete Steiff ca. 1898. **85** Margarete Steiff 1905. **86 & 87** Swaine & Co. **88** Thüringer Puppen- und Spielwaren-Export GmbH 1923. **89** Gustav Thiele. **90** Friedr. Edmund Winkler 1899.

Circles	Ovals (Upright)	Triangles

91 Adolf Wislizenus 1902. **92** Emil Wittzack. **93** A. C. Anger, Böhmen. **94** unknown.

91 92 93 94

1 Max Göhring 1924. **2** Henze & Steinhäuser 1912. **3** Edmund Knoch. **4** Müller & Kaltwasser. **5** Paul Schmidt 1922.

1 2 3

4 5

1 Oskar Büchner. **2** Concentra. **3** Christian Eichhorn & Söhne.

1 2 3

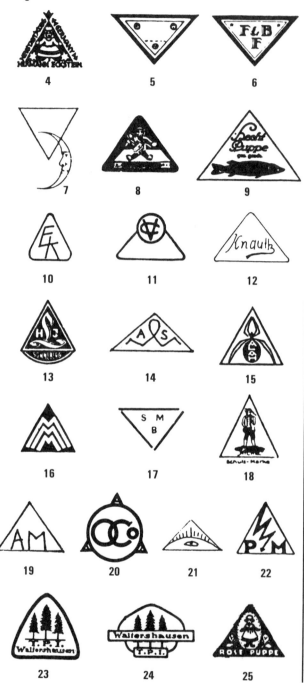

4 Hermann Eckstein. **5** Fleischmann & Bloedel 1895. **6** Fleischmann & Bloedel at the end of 1920's. **7** F. W. Goebel. **8** Carl Harmus 1905. **9** Else L. Hecht. **10** Erich Klötzer. **11** Kloster Veilsdorf. **12** Guido Knauth. **13** H.J. Leven. **14** Limbach AG. **15** Anni Lonz 1924. **16** Ma. E. Maar. **17** Sigismund Markmann. **18** Amandus Michaelis 1911. **19** Amandus Michaelis. **20** H. Offenbacher & Co. **21** Gebr. Ohlhaver (see Porzellanfabrik Mengersgereuth). **22** Porzellanfabrik Mengersgereuth. **23 & 24** Thüringer Puppen-Industrie 1923. **25** F. Welsch 1925.

Ovals (Laying)

1 Canzler & Hoffman 1925. **2** Christan Eichhorn & Söhne. **3** C. Erich Günther 1922. **4** Gebr. Haag 1886. **5** Therese Heininger 1925. **6** Sommer & Co. GmbH. **7** Karl Standuss. **8** Erste Steinbacher Porzellanfabrik. **9** Louis Wolf & Co.

Diamond - Shapes

1   2   3

4   5   6

7   8   9

1 Deutsche Kolonial-Kapok-Werke 1925. **2** Hermann Eckstein. **3** A. Fleischmann & Craemer 1881. **4** Carl Geyer. **5** Gebr. Haag after 1920. **6** Hammer Munitionswerk 1920. **7** Dr. Paul Huneaus 1901. **8** Richard Leutheuser. **9** Armand Marseille for C.M. Bergmann 1904.

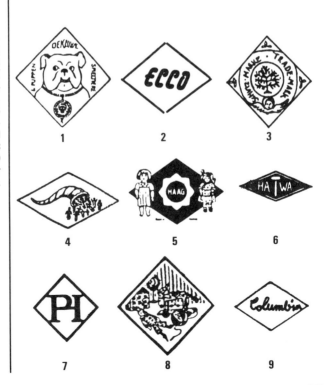

1   2   3

4   5   6

7   8   9

10

11

12

13

14

15

16

17

18

19

10 Armand Marseille for unknown firm. **11** Rauch & Schelhorn. **12** Rheinische Gummi- und Celluloidwaren-Fabrik after 1909. **13** A. Riedeler. **14** Arthur Schoenau 1913. **15** E.U. Steiner. **16** Sigismund Ullmann 1922. **17** Vereinigte Köppelsdorfer Porzellanfabriken. **18** Waltershäuser Puppenfabrik 1921. **19** Otto Wohlmann 1908.

1

2

3

4

5

6

7

8

1 Edgard Goldstein & Co. 1919. **2** Hahn & Co. 1921. **3** Max Handwerck 1901. **4** Carl Hartmann 1898. **5** Friedrich A. Heubach Succes. 1920. **6** Werner Krauth 1920. **7** Louis Lindner & Söhne. **8** Karl Pietsch.

1 Louis Wolf & Co. **2** Geo. Borgfeldt & Co. 1903, with "Real Hair Eyebrows" 1910. **3** Hamburger & Co. 1901. **4** Sears, Roebuck & Co., made by an unknown firm. **5** Butler Brothers GmbH. 1913 (also used with "Non Plus Ultra"). **6** Cuno & Otto Dressel 1912. **7** J.D. Kestner jr. **8** unknown presumably made by a Sonneberg firm. **9 & 10** labels made by different firms "Cork-oder Hair-Stuffed". **11 & 12** Fischer, Naumann & Co. **13** Wagner & Zetsche.

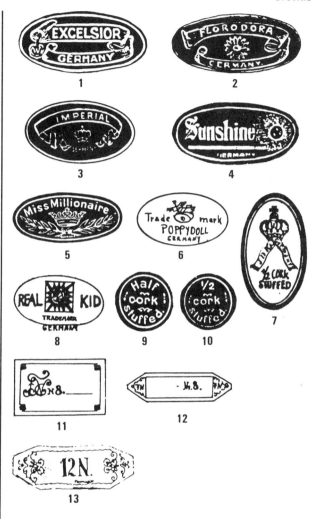

1 F&W. Goebel. **2** Heber & Co. **3** J.D. Kestner jr. 1915

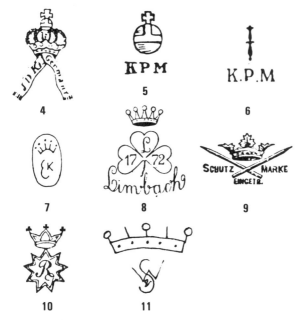

4 J. D. Kestner jr. 1896. 5 Königl. Porzellanmanufaktur Berlin 1832. 6 Königl. Porzellanmanufaktur 1837. 7 Edmund Knoch. 8 Limbach AG. 9 Andreas Müller 1896. 10 Schäfer & Vater. 11 Walther & Sohn.

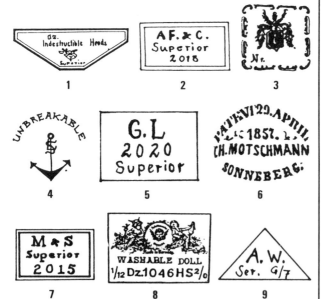

1 Cuno & Otto Dressel. 2 A. Fleischmann & Craemer. 3 Samuel Krauss 1875 (only found on figurines made of papier-mache). 4 Lambert & Samhammer 1870. 5 Georg Lutz ca. 1887. 6 Christoph Motschmann 1857. 7 Müller & Strasburger. 8 F. M. Schillig 1879. 9 Adolf Wislizenus.

10 Adolf Wislizenus. **11 & 12** unknown, found on papier-mâché heads with molded hair.

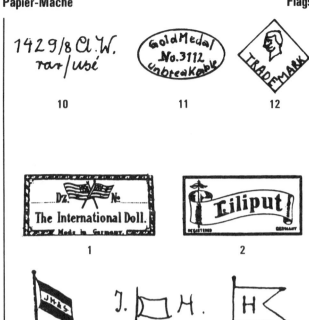

10   11   12

1 Geo. Borgfeldt & Co. **2** Carl Geyer 1902. **3 & 4** Hering & Sohn. **5** Ernst Heubach. **6** Keramisches Werk Gräfenhain. **7** Kley & Hahn. **8** M. Kohnstamm & Co. **9** Mimosa 1923. **10** Louis Wolf & Co. **11** Kohler & Rosenwald 1927. **12** Hermann Landshut & Co. 1895.

1   2

3   4   5

6   7   8

9   10

11   12

1 Resi Brandl 1924. **2** Oskar Büchner. **3** Josef Deuerlein Succes. 1904. **4** Josef Deuerlein Succes. 1925. **5** Deutsche Kolonial-Kapok-Werke 1925. **6** Dressel & Pietschmann. **7** Fleischmann & Bloedel 1914. **8** Albert Förster. **9** Hahn & Co. **10** Carl Harmus Jr. 1909. **11** Else L. Hecht. **12** Henze & Steinhäuser 1925. **13** Hermsdorfer Celluloidwarenfabrik. **14** Hering & Sohn. **15** Hertwig & Co. **16** Hugo Heubach. **17** Martin Winterbauer. **18** Kohler & Rosenwald.

Animals

19 Louis Philipp Luthardt. **20** Edith Maus 1925. **21 & 22** Rheinische Gummi- und Celluloid-Fabrik used since 1889 in various kinds. **23** Heinrich Schmuckler 1921. **24** Wilhelm Simon 1875. **25** Margarete Steiff ca. 1892. **26** Margarete Steiff ca. 1898. **27** Erste Steinnbacher Porzellanfabrik. **28** Wilhelm Strunz. **29** Heinrich Weiss 1895. **30** Otto Wohlmann 1908. **31** Hermann Wolf 1923. **32** Gebr. Wolff.

1 Richard Beck & Co. **2** Johannes Franz 1858. **3** Delly-Puppenfabrik 1925.

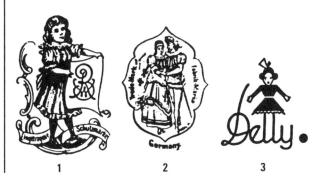

4 Gutmann & Schiffnie 1911. **5** Berthold Helk 1927. **6** Herzpuppen-Fabrik 1923. **7** Albin Hess 1930. **8** Huttinger & Buschor 1921. **9** Marion Kaulitz 1909. **10** Arthur Laufer 1925. **11** Anton Link 1924. **12** Leo Nordschild 1924. **13** Gebr. Paris 1907. **14** Puppen-Industrie Gotha 1924. **15** Rotkäppchen GmbH. 1925. **16** Richard Scherzer 1924. **17** Rudolf Schneider 1914. **18** Simon & Halbig 1875.

Trademarks

Hearts

19 Max Spindler. **20** Hermann Steiner, Neustadt 1927. **21** Hermann Steiner Sonneberg. **22** Josef Strasser 1922. **23** Gebr. Süssenguth 1909 and Gutmann & Schiffnie 1907. **24** Paul Wernicke 1925. **25** H. Wordtmann, Hamburg. **26** Württembergische Spielwarenfabrik 1924. **27** Edmund Carl Zehner 1924. **28** P.R. Zierow 1910.

1 Baehr & Proeschild. **2** Albin Hess. **3 & 4** labels for Kewpies. **5** Porzellanfabrik Mengersgereuth. **6** A. Reideler. **7 & 8** Bruno Schmidt. **9** Arthur Schoenau.

23

Cloverleaves	Helmets	Eagles

1 Bühl & Söhne. **2** Kloster Veilsdorf. **3-5** Limbach AG. **6** Hermann Pensky. **7** Adolf Wislizenus

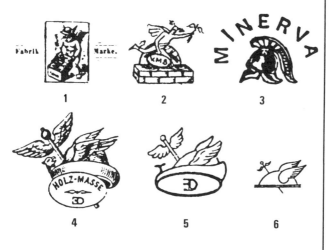

1 Max Oscar Arnold. **2** V.M. Bruchlos. **3** Buschow & Beck 1900. **4-6** Cuno & Otto Dressel.

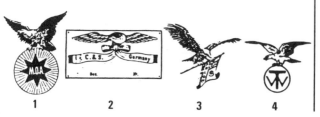

1 Max Oscar Arnold. **2** Curnen & Steiner 1898. **3** Otto Schamberger. **4** Theodor Wendt 1924.

Birds

Anchors

1 Otto Gans. **2** Paul Hausmeister & Co. **3** Jacob Jung 1912. **4 & 5** August Luge & Co. **6** Schwäbische Celluloidwaren-Fabrik. **7** Emil Schwenk. **8** Sigismund Schwerin Nachf. 1923.

1 Johann Philipp Dressel. **2** Lambert & Samhammer 1876. **3** Armand Marseille ca. 1893. **4** Armand Marseille for Louis Wolf & Co. 1896. **5** Armand Marseille ca. 1910. **6** Armand Marseille 1910. **7** Armand Marseille 1920. **8** Möller & Dippe. **9** Emil Zitzmann 1913.

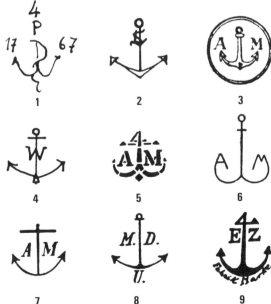

Hammers, Anvils, Nails

Suns

1 Gebr. Metzler & Ortloff. **2 & 3** Theodor Recknagel. **4-8** various trademarks of Franz Schmidt & Co.

1 Emil Bauersachs. **2** Fleischmann & Craemer. **3** Porzellanfabrik Mengersgereuth 1908. **4 & 5** Gebr. Heubach. **6** Carl A. Illing & Co.

Suns

7 Gebr. Kühnlenz. **8** A. Luge & Co. 1926. **9** Heinrich Liebermann 1927. **10** Morgenroth & Co. **11** W.G. Müller. **12** Müller & Fröbel. **13** Gebr. Ohlhaver. **14** Preussig & Wilson 1914. **15** Paul Schmidt 1923. **16** Seyfarth & Reinhardt 1923. **17** Sigismund Ullmann 1926. **18** Friedrich Voigt. **19** Welsch & Co.

1 L. Bierer. **2** Bing Künstlerpuppen und Stoffspielwarengesellschaft. **3** Cuno & Otto Dressel 1907.

Heads	**Swords**	**Horseshoes, Arcs, Trains**

4 Thüringer Puppen-industrie 1923. **5** F. M. Schilling.

1 Baehr & Proeschild. **2** Dornheim. Koch & Fischer. **3** Theodor Degenring. **4** Königl. Porzellanmanufaktur Meissen. **5** Porzellan-fabrik Rauenstein. **6** Theodor Pohl, Böh-men.

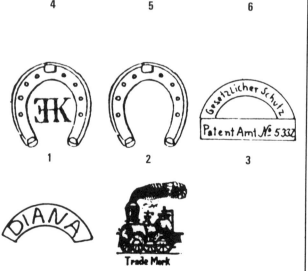

1 & 2 Ernst Heubach. **3** Johannes Franz 1892. **4** Alfred Heller 1903. **5** E. Escher Jun. 1896.

Coat-of-Arms

Bells

1 Cellba Celluloid-warenfabrik. 2 Conta & Böhme. 3 Berthold Eck 1876. 4 Otto Gans. 5 Gebr. Heubach. 6 Hermann Heyde 1910. 7 Königl. Bayer. Porzellan-Manufaktur. 8 Samuel Krauss 1875. 9 Sonneberger Porzellanfabrik Carl Müller. 10 Theodor Recknagel. 11 Max Friedrich Schelhorn 1908. 12 Arthur Schoenau. 13 Unger & Schilde. 14 Zeuch & Lausmann 1895. 15 heraldic figure of Sonneberg.

1 Geo. Borgfeldt & Co. 2 C.F. Kling. 3 presumably C.F. Kling for K&R. 4 Nöckler & Tittel.

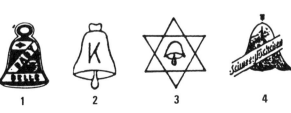

29

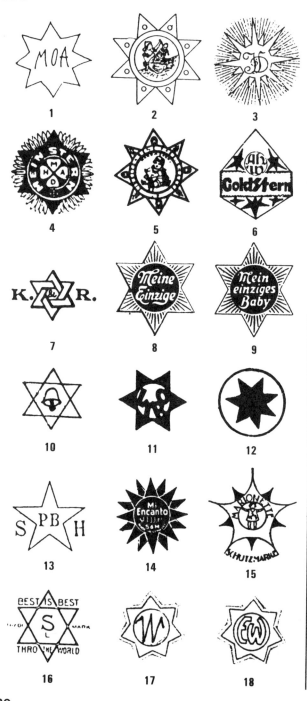

1 Max Oscar Arnold.
2 C.M. Bergmann ca.
1926. 3 Julius Dorst
1895. 4 Henriette
Dunker 1923. 5 Heinrich Handwerck 1891
(used on trademarks
"Bebe Cosmopolite"
and "Bebe de Reclame"). 6 Adolf Hülss
1925. 7 Kämmer &
Reinhardt 1896. 8 Kley
& Hahn 1910. 9 Kley
& Hahn 1913. 10 presumable C.F. Kling for
K&R. 11 Lyro-Puppen-
Company 1923 and
Rolfes & Co. 1923. 12
Moritz Pappe 1907. 13
Schoenau & Hoffmeister. 14 Seligmann
& Mayer 1930. 15
Mylius Sperschneider
1922. 16 Josef Süsskind. 17 Ernst Winkler
1910. 18 Ernst
Winkler 1925.

Stars

19 P.R. Zierow 1914. **20** Gottlieb Zinner & Söhne. **21** Cuno & Otto Dressel. **22** Erich von Berg. **23** unknown. **24** Armand Marseille for unknown firm.

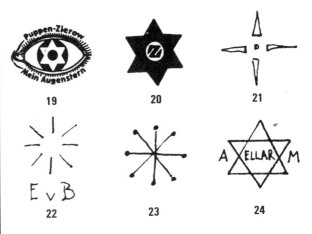

19

20

21

22

23

24

1 Alt, Beck & Gottschalck. **2** Julius Dorst. **3 & 4** Cuno & Otto Dressel. **5** Fischer, Naumann & Co. **6** Otto Gans. **7** Greif-Puppenkunst. **8** Greiner & Co. **9** Heber & Co. **10** Carl Hartmann. **11** Hertwig & Co. **12** Gebr. Heubach.

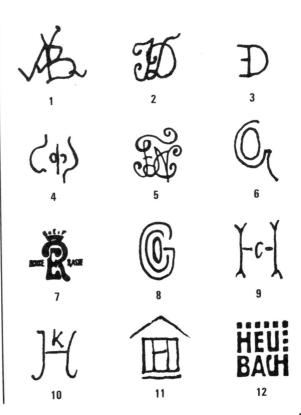

1

2

3

4

5

6

7

8

9

10

11

12

13 Carl Horn Succes.
14 Dr. Paul Huneaus.
15 & 16 Kestner &
Co. **17** Kloster Veils-
dorf. **18** Gebr. Knoch.
19 Kohl & Wengen-
roth. **20** Gustav Korn.
21 Gebr. Kühnlenz.
22 Marienfeld. **23**
Carl Moritz. **24** Karl
Müller & Co. **25** Niko-
laus Oberender. **26**
Emil Pfeifer. **27** Fritz
Pfeiffer. **28** Max Ru-
dolph. **29** August
Schellhorn. **30** Carl
Schneider Erben. **31**
Schützmeister &
Quendt. **32 & 33**
Hermann Steiner.

Ciphers

34 Hermann Steiner.
35 Gebr. Süssenguth.
36 Strobel & Wilken.
37 & 38 Gebr. Voigt
(No. 38 also see Alt,
Beck & Gottschalck).
39 Wagner & Zetsche.
40 Walther & Sohn.
41 Johann Walter. **42**
presumably Theodor
Wendt. **43** Gustav
Wohlleben. **44** Carl
Knoll, Böhmen. **45**
Weiskirchlitzer Stein-
gutfabrik, Böhmen. **46**
Gustav Thiele.

Wreaths

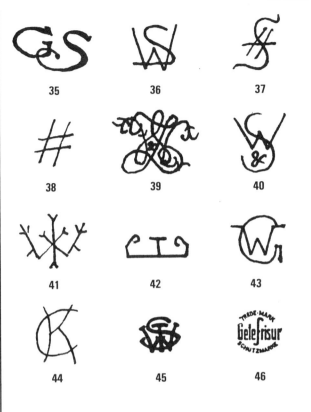

1 Emil Bauersachs
1895. **2** Fleischmann
& Bloedel 1890. **3** Dr.
Paul Huneaus. **4** Jo-
hann Heinrich Kletzin
& Co. **5** Nöckler &
Tittel.

Mold No.	Firm	Date	Description and Identification
13	Gebr. Kühnlenz	ca 1885	dolly face, mold number with hyphen and size number, **ill. 1083**
21	Gebr. Kühnlenz	GM 1891	dolly face
22	Theodor Recknagel	GM 1912	character, girl with molded bonnet, painted eyes, open/closed laughing mouth, **ill. 1440**
23	Theodor Recknagel	GM 1912	character
24	Theodor Recknagel	GM 1912	character
25	Theodor Recknagel	GM 1912	character
26	Theodor Recknagel	GM 1912	character
27	Theodor Recknagel	GM 1912	character
28	Theodor Recknagel	GM 1912	character, boy with molded cap, painted eyes, open/closed laughing mouth, **ill. 1439**
29	Theodor Recknagel	GM 1912	"RA", character, girl with molded bonnet and blue ribbon, painted eyes, open/closed laughing mouth
	Gebr. Kühnlenz	GM 1891	dolly face
30	Theodor Recknagel	GM 1912	character
	F&W. Goebel	ca 1890	shoulder head, glass eyes, closed mouth
31	Theodor Recknagel	GM 1912	character, Max, **ill. 1445**
	unknown	ca 1890	"dep", shoulder head, molded hair, painted eyes, closed mouth

Mold No.	Firm	Date	Description and Identification
31	unknown	ca 1890	"B Germany", shoulder head, molded hair, glass eyes, closed mouth
32	Theodor Recknagel	GM 1912	character, Moritz
	Gebr. Kühnlenz	ca 1890	dolly face, mold number with hyphen and size No., ill. 1082
33	Theodor Recknagel	GM 1914	character
34	Theodor Recknagel	GM 1914	character, mold number with hyphen and size no., presumably coloured compo, glass eyes, open mouth, Black Doll or Mulatto
	F&W. Goebel	GM 1887	dolly face
35	Theodor Recknagel	GM 1914	character
37	Theodor Recknagel	GM 1914	character
39	Theodor Recknagel	GM 1914	character
40	Max Räder	GM 1910	"dep.", dolly face
41	Theodor Recknagel	GM 1914	character
43	Theodor Recknagel	GM 1914	character, boy with molded cap
44	Theodor Recknagel	GM 1914	character, with painted googly eyes
	Gebr. Kühnlenz	GM 1895	"dep" or "GK" or "Gebr.K.", dolly face, ill. 1084
45	Theodor Recknagel	ca 1914	character
46	F&W. Goebel	GM 1888	dolly face

Mold No.	Firm	Date	Description and Identification
47	Theodor Recknagel	GM 1914	character, painted googly eyes, ill. 1442
	Max Räder	ca 1910	"R-DEP", shoulder head, dolly face, ill. 1432
48	Theodor Recknagel	GM 1914	character
49	Theodor Recknagel	GM 1914	character
50	Theodor Recknagel	GM 1914	"AR DEP", character
	Max Räder	GM 1910	"R.DEP", dolly face, mold number with hyphen and size no., ill. 1433 + 1434
	F&W. Goebel	ca 1910	"WG" with crown, character with painted eyes
53	Theodor Recknagel	GM 1914	character
54	Theodor Recknagel	GM 1914	character with painted googly eyes
	F&W. Goebel	GM 1887	presumably dolly face
	Max Oscar Arnold	ca 1909	"54/14" (Arnoldia), dolly face, ill. 41 + 1737 + 1738
55	Theodor Recknagel	GM 1914	character, solid dome, molded hair, painted eyes, open/ closed laughing mouth, upper 2 painted teeth, Black Doll
56	Theodor Recknagel	GM 1914	character
	Gebr. Kühnlenz	ca 1900	dolly face
58	Theodor Recknagel	GM 1914	character
60	F&W. Goebel	ca 1900	dolly face
68	Gebr. Kühnlenz	GM 1889	dolly face

Mold No.	Firm	Date	Description and Identification
69	Heinrich Handwerck	ca 1900	dolly face
71	Gebr. Kühnlenz	GM 1889	shoulder head, dolly face, mold number with hyphen and size number
72	Gebr. Kühnlenz	GM 1889	dolly face
73	Theodor Recknagel	ca 1915	grotesque head with big eyes
	F&W. Goebel	ca 1914	girl with molded hair and flowers, painted eyes
75	Gebr. Kühnlenz	GM 1889	dolly face
76	Gebr. Kühnlenz	GM 1889	dolly face
77	Gebr. Kühnlenz	GM 1889	dolly face
	F&W. Goebel	ca 1914	head with molded military cap
	Seyfarth & Reinhardt	GM 1925	character
79	Heinrich Handwerck	ca 1900	dolly face, ill. 553
	Schützmeister & Quendt	GM 1891	dolly face
80	Schützmeister & Quendt	GM 1891	dolly face
	F&W. Goebel	ca 1914	character, called "Walter"
81	Schützmeister & Quendt	GM 1891	dolly face
82	F&W. Goebel	ca 1914	head with molded German military cap
83	F&W. Goebel	ca 1914	head with molded Austrian military cap
84	F&W. Goebel	ca 1914	"WG", head with molded Bulgarian military cap, ill. color 42

Mold No.	Firm	Date	Description and Identification
85	F&W. Goebel	ca 1914	head with molded Turkey military cap
86	F&W. Goebel	ca 1914	head without cap
	Theodor Recknagel	ca 1915	character baby
87	F&W. Goebel	ca 1914	head with molded German military cap
88	F&W. Goebel	ca 1914	head with molded Austrian military cap
89	F&W. Goebel	ca 1914	socket head
	Heinrich Handwerck	ca 1890	dolly face, **ill. 546 + 86 + 87 + 88**
90	F&W. Goebel	ca 1900	"B/90/185", for Max Handwerck, dolly face
91	F&W. Goebel	ca 1914	character
92	F&W. Goebel	GM 1914	character
93	Armand Marseille	GM 1892	"COD", for Cuno & Otto Dressel, shoulder head (mold number abbreviation for the year 18<u>93</u>)
98	Hertel, Schwab & Co.	ca 1910	"made in Germany", for Koenig & Wernicke, character
99	Hertel, Schwab & Co.	ca 1910	"made in Germany", for Koenig & Wernicke, character also as Black Doll
	Heinrich Handwerck	ca 1900	"DEP", dolly face
100	Kämmer & Reinhardt	GM 1909	"K&R", Baby, character, solid dome, painted eyes, open/closed mouth, also as Black Doll or Oriental, rare version with glass eyes and wig, **ill. 802**

Mold No.	Firm	Date	Description and Identification
100	Arno Frank	GM 1902	dollhead with molded glass eye brows
	Peter Scherf	GM 1916	character
	A.Möller & Sohn	ca 1915	"Amuso", dolly face
	unknown	ca 1880	"Elsa", dolly face,solid dome, glass eyes, closed mouth
101	Kämmer & Reinhardt	GM 1909	"K&R", Peter or Marie, character, painted eyes,closed mouth, rare version with glass eyes, also as Black Doll, ill. 803
	Theodor Recknagel	ca 1900	marked with the head of a moor, for L. Bierer, dolly face, ill. 139
	Peter Scherf	GM 1916	character
	Schützmeister & Quendt	ca 1900	"SQ", dolly face
	B.Illfelder & Co.	ca 1908	"AW.My Sweetheart B.I.& Co" dolly face
102	Kämmer & Reinhardt	GM 1909	"K&R", Elsa or Walter, character, molded hair painted eyes, closed mouth, ill. 804
	Peter Scherf	GM 1916	character
	Schützmeister & Quendt	ca 1900	dolly face
	F&W. Goebel	ca 1910	character, solid dome, sleep eyes, closed mouth
103	Kämmer & Reinhardt	ca 1909	"K&R", character, painted eyes, closed mouth, ill. 805
	Peter Scherf	GM 1916	character
	unknown	ca 1890	dolly face, glass eyes, closed mouth
104	Kämmer & Reinhardt	ca 1909	"K&R", character, painted eyes, laughing, closed mouth

Mold No.	Firm	Date	Description and Identification
104	Theodor Recknagel	ca 1915	"RA DEP", character, shoulder head with molded hair, painted eyes, closed mouth
	Hertwig & Co.	ca 1890	shoulder head with a molded flower as hat, painted features
	unknown	ca 1880	socket head, solid dome with 3 holes, painted or glass eyes, closed mouth
105	Kämmer & Reinhardt	ca 1909	"K&R", character, painted eyes, open/closed mouth, **ill. 806**
	Theodor Recknagel	ca 1915	character, shoulder head
106	Kämmer & Reinhardt	GM 1909	"K&R", character, painted eyes, slightly open mouth, **ill. 807**
	F&W. Goebel	1921-32	character
107	Kämmer & Reinhardt	GM 1909	"K&R", Carl, character, painted eyes, closed mouth, **ill. 808**
	F&W. Goebel	1921-32	character
108	Kämmer & Reinhardt	ca 1909	character, no further information
109	Kämmer & Reinhardt	GM 1909	"K&R", Elise, character, painted or glass eyes, closed mouth
	Heinrich Handwerck	ca 1900	dolly face, **ill. color 2 + ill. 551 + 555**
110	Kämmer & Reinhardt	GM 1909	character, no further information
	unknown	ca 1910	character, solid dome, painted eyes, open/closed mouth, for Carl Debes & Sohn, **ill. 239**, and for Adolf Wislizenus, **ill. 1974**

Mold No.	Firm	Date	Description and Identification
110	F&W. Goebel	1921-32	character
111	Kämmer & Reinhardt	GM 1909	character, no further information
	F&W. Goebel	1921-32	character
	unknown	ca 1880	socket head, solid dome with 3 holes, glass eyes, closed mouth
112	Kämmer & Reinhardt	GM 1909	"K&R", character, painted or glass eyes, open/closed mouth
114	Kämmer & Reinhardt	GM 1909	"K&R", Hans or Gretchen, character. painted or sleep eyes, closed mouth, ill. 809
	F&W. Goebel	1921-32	character
	Porzellanfabrik Rauenstein	ca 1890	china shoulder head with molded hair, painted features
115	Kämmer & Reinhardt	GM 1911	"S&H/K&R", character, solid dome, sleep eyes, closed mouth
115A	Kämmer & Reinhardt	GM 1911	"S&H/K&R", character, sleep eyes, closed mouth, wig, ill. 810
116	Kämmer & Reinhardt	GM 1911	"S&H/K&R", character, solid dome, sleep eyes, open/closed mouth
	C.F. Kling	ca 1880	shoulder head with molded hair and hat, glass eyes, closed mouth
116A	Kämmer & Reinhardt	GM 1911	"S&H/K&R", character, sleep eyes, open/closed or open mouth, wig, ill. 811
117	Kämmer & Reinhardt	GM 1911	"S&H/K&R" Mein Liebling, character, glass eyes, closed mouth, rare version with open mouth, ill. 812

Mold No.	Firm	Date	Description and Identification
117A	Kämmer & Reinhardt	GM 1911	"S&H/K&R", character, glass eyes, closed mouth
117X	Kämmer & Reinhardt	GM 1911	"S&H/K&R", character, presumably lower size no. of mold number 117
117n	Kämmer & Reinhardt	GM 1916	"S&H/K&R", Mein neuer Liebling, character, sleep eyes, open mouth
118	Kämmer & Reinhardt	ca 1911	"S&H/K&R", character, sleep eyes, open mouth
118A	Kämmer & Reinhardt	ca 1911	"S&H/K&R", character, sleep eyes, open mouth, ill. 813
118	unknown	ca 1890	shoulder head, glass eyes, open mouth, dolly face, presumable Kestner
119	Kämmer & Reinhardt	ca 1913	"S&H/K&R", baby, character, sleep eyes, open/closed mouth, ill. 814
	Heinrich Handwerck	ca 1900	dolly face, ill. 549
	C.F. Kling	ca 1880	shoulder head with molded hair, glass eyes, closed mouth.
120	Kämmer & Reinhardt	ca 1915	"S&H", character, sleep eyes, open mouth, ill. 815
	F&W. Goebel	1921-32	character, sleep eyes, open mouth
	Max Friedr. Schelhorn	GM 1912	character, multi-face
	J.D. Kestner jr.	GM 1897	dolly face
121	Kämmer & Reinhardt	GM 1912	"K&R", character, sleep eyes, open mouth, ill. 816
	F&W. Goebel	1921-32	character
	Max Friedr. Schelhorn	GM 1912	character, multi-face

Mold No.	Firm	Date	Description and Identification
121	Theodor Recknagel	ca 1905	dolly face
	unknown	ca 1900	marked with crown, dolly face
	unknown	ca 1880	socket head, solid dome with 3 holes, closed mouth, ill. 2033
	J.D. Kestner jr.	GM 1897	dolly face
122	Kämmer & Reinhardt	GM 1912	"S&H/K&R", character, sleep eyes, open mouth, ill. 817
	Max Friedr. Schelhorn	GM 1912	character, multi-face
	F&W. Goebel	1921-32	presumably character
	C.F. Kling	GM 1881	shoulder head with molded hair, glass eyes, closed mouth
	unknown	ca 1900	"M", dolly face
	J.D. Kestner jr.	GM 1897	dolly face
123	Kämmer & Reinhardt	GM 1913	"S&H/K&R", character, Max, flirting sleep eyes, laughing, closed mouth, ill. 793
	Max Friedr. Schelhorn	GM 1912	character, multi-face
	F&W. Goebel	1921-32	character
	C.F. Kling	ca 1880	incised bell, shoulder head, glass eyes, closed mouth
	J.D. Kestner jr.	GM 1897	dolly face
124	Kämmer & Reinhardt	GM 1913	"S&H/K&R", character, Moritz, flirting sleep eyes, laughing closed mouth, ill. 792
	F&W. Goebel	1921-32	character
	C.F. Kling	ca 1880	incised bell, shoulder head, sleep eyes, open mouth, ill. color 88
	unknown	ca 1900	"WD" with crown, dolly face
	J.D. Kestner jr.	GM 1897	dolly face

Mold No.	Firm	Date	Description and Identification
125	Kämmer & Reinhardt	ca 1914	character, no further information
	unknown	ca 1914	character, sleep eyes, smiling mouth, presumably K&R
	F&W. Goebel	1921-32	presumably character
	Nikolaus Oberender	ca 1910	"NO", character, sleep eyes, open mouth, ill. 1335
	unknown	ca 1890	shoulder head, china, molded hair, painted features
	J.D. Kestner jr.	GM 1897	dolly face
126	Kämmer & Reinhardt	1914	"S&H/K&R", Mein Lieblings-Baby character, sleep or flirting eyes, bent-limb baby or toddler, ill. color 70 - 73, also all-biskuit bent-limb body marked with "1126-19"
	Hertel, Schwab & Co.	ca 1912	character, solid dome with painted hair, sleep eyes, open mouth, Skippy
	Eisenmann & Co.	GM 1913	character
	F&W. Goebel	1921-32	character
	Walther & Sohn	ca 1920	character, socket head
	Theodor Recknagel	ca 1925	newborn, flange neck, sleep eyes, closed mouth, ill. 1443
	J.D. Kestner jr.	GM 1897	dolly face
127	Kämmer & Reinhardt	GM 1914	"K&R", character, solid dome, sleep eyes, open mouth (same model as mold # 126)
	Hertel, Schwab & Co.	ca 1915	character, solid dome with molded hair, sleep eyes, open mouth, Patsy
	presumable Hertel, Schwab & Co.	ca 1915	character, solid dome with painted eyes, open/closed, smiling mouth
	Theodor Recknagel	ca 1925	newborn, flange neck, sleep eyes, closed mouth, Black Doll, ill. 1446

Mold No.	Firm	Date	Description and Identification
127	J.D. Kestner jr.	GM 1897	dolly face
128	Kämmer & Reinhardt	GM 1914	character, sleep eyes, open mouth
	Hermann Steiner	ca 1920	"HS", character
	C.F. Kling	ca 1880	shoulder head with molded hair and black comb, glass eyes closed mouth, ill. color 79
	Theodor Recknagel	GM 1925	baby with one tooth
	J.D. Kestner jr.	GM 1897	dolly face
129	Hertel, Schwab & Co.	ca 1910	"made in Germany", character, sleep eyes, closed mouth
	Sonneberger Porzellanfabrik	ca 1900	"SP", dolly face
	C.F. Kling	ca 1880	shoulder head, china or bisque, with molded hair, painted eyes, closed mouth
	Theodor Recknagel	GM 1925	baby with two teeth
	J.D. Kestner jr.	GM 1897	dolly face, ill. 863 – 867
130	Wiesenthal, Schindel & Kallenberg	ca 1912	"WSK", character, painted eyes, open/closed mouth
	Max Oscar Arnold	ca 1920	"MOA", character
	Hertel, Schwab & Co.	ca 1912	character, sleep eyes, open/closed mouth
	C.F. Kling	ca 1885	incised bell, shoulder head, glass eyes, closed mouth
	J.D. Kestner jr.	ca 1897	dolly face
131	Kämmer & Reinhardt	ca 1914	"S&H/K&R", character, googly eyes, closed mouth, ill. 832
	C.F. Kling	ca 1885	incised bell, shoulder head, china, with molded hair, painted features or other version in bisque, glass eyes, closed mouth

Mold No.	Firm	Date	Description and Identification
131	Hertel, Schwab & Co.	ca 1912	character, solid dome, painted eyes, closed mouth
	Theodor Recknagel	GM 1926	baby
	J.D. Kestner jr.	GM 1897	dolly face
132	Kämmer & Reinhardt	GM 1921	character
	Hertel, Schwab & Co.	ca 1912	"made in Germany", character, sleep eyes, open mouth with tongue
	Theodor Recknagel	GM 1926	baby
	J.D. Kestner jr.	GM 1897	dolly face
133	Kämmer & Reinhardt	GM 1923	character
	Hermann Steiner	ca 1920	"HS", character, googly eyes, closed mouth
	Hugo Wiegand	ca 1920	"HW", character,
	Hertel, Schwab & Co.	ca 1912	character, solid dome, painted eyes, closed mouth, for Kley & Hahn
	C.F. Kling	ca 1885	shoulder head with molded hair, glass eyes, closed mouth
	J.D. Kestner jr.	GM 1897	dolly face
134	Keramisches Werk	ca 1932	"KWG", character, compo
	Hermann Steiner	ca 1920	"HS", Black Doll
	Hertel, Schwab & Co.	ca 1915	character, sleep eyes, closed mouth
	Theodor Recknagel	GM 1926	baby
	J.D. Kestner jr.	GM 1897	dolly face
135	Kämmer & Reinhardt	ca 1923	character, sleep eyes, open mouth
	Hertel, Schwab & Co.	ca 1912	character, solid dome, painted eyes, open/closed mouth, for Kley & Hahn, ill. 935

Mold No.	Firm	Date	Description and Identification
135	Theodor Recknagel	GM 1926	baby
	C.F. Kling	ca 1885	shoulder head, molded hair, molded blouse, painted eyes, closed mouth, or other version with molded flowers and glass eyes
	J.D. Kestner jr.	GM 1897	dolly face
136	Hertel, Schwab & Co.	ca 1912	"made in Germany", character, sleep eyes, open mouth
	Keramisches Werk	ca 1932	"KWG", character, compo
	unknown	ca 1905	socket head, glass eyes, closed mouth
	Theodor Recknagel	GM 1926	baby
	J.D. Kestner jr.	GM 1897	dolly face, glass eyes, closed mouth
137	Theodor Recknagel	ca 1925	newborn, flange neck sleep eyes, closed mouth
	J.D. Kestner jr.	GM 1897	dolly face, solid dome, glass eyes, closed mouth
138	Hertel, Schwab & Co.	ca 1912	character, solid dome, painted or sleep eyes, open/closed mouth with molded tongue, for Kley & Hahn
	Theodor Recknagel	ca 1925	"RA", newborn, flange neck or socket head, glass eyes, closed mouth, also as Black Doll
	J.D. Kestner jr.	GM 1897	dolly face
139	Heinrich Handwerck	ca 1900	dolly face
	J.D. Kestner jr.	GM 1897	dolly face
140	Hertel, Schwab & Co.	ca 1912	character, glass eyes, open/closed mouth, laughing
	C.F. Kling	ca 1885	shoulder head, molded hair boy, glass eyes, closed mouth

Mold No.	Firm	Date	Description and Identification
140	unknown	ca 1890	shoulder head with molded cut-out for wig, glass eyes, closed mouth, ill. 2034 + 2049 + 2050
	J.D. Kestner jr.	GM 1897	dolly face
141	Hertel, Schwab & Co.	ca 1912	character, painted eyes, open/closed mouth, ill. 626
	C.F. Kling	GM 1881	head
	J.D. Kestner jr.	GM 1897	dolly face
142	Kämmer & Reinhardt	ca 1923	"S&H/K&R", character baby, sleep eyes, open mouth
	Hertel, Schwab & Co.	ca 1912	character, solid dome, painted or sleep eyes, open/closed mouth or open mouth with molded tongue, ill. 1901
	Geo. Borgfeldt & Co.	GM 1925	crawling baby, character
	C.F. Kling	GM 1881	head
	J.D. Kestner jr.	GM 1897	dolly face
143	Hertel, Schwab & Co.	ca 1912	character, glass eyes, closed smiling mouth with teeth
	J.D. Kestner jr.	GM 1897	dolly face
144	Kämmer & Reinhardt	ca 1920	"K&R", character, painted eyes, closed mouth
	J.D. Kestner jr.	GM 1897	dolly face
145	J.D. Kestner jr.	GM 1897	dolly face
146	J.D. Kestner jr.	GM 1897	dolly face
147	Hertel, Schwab & Co.	ca 1914	character, googly eyes, open/closed mouth
	J.D. Kestner jr.	ca 1897	shoulder head, dolly face

Mold No.	Firm	Date	Description and Identification
148	Hertel, Schwab & Co.	ca 1910	character, glass eyes, open/closed mouth, crying with real tears, produced by rubberball-mechanism, ill. 1513 + 1514
	C.F. Kling	ca 1885	shoulder head, molded hair painted eyes, closed mouth
	J.D. Kestner jr.	ca 1897	shoulder head, dolly face
149	Hertel, Schwab & Co.	ca 1912	character, sleep or painted eyes, closed mouth
	J.D. Kestner jr.	ca 1897	dolly face
150	Hertel, Schwab & Co.	ca 1912	character, solid dome or cut out for wig, painted or sleep eyes, open/closed or open mouth with tongue ill. 629
	Hertel, Schwab & Co.	ca 1911	"WSK-DRGM-452711", character sleep eyes, open/closed mouth, for Wiesenthal, Schindel & Kallenberg, ill. 1940
	Simon & Halbig	ca 1912	character, painted eyes, closed mouth, ill. 1697
	Max Oscar Arnold	ca 1920	"MOA-Welsch", character, for Welsch & Co.
	Gebr. Ohlhaver	ca 1920	character
	Hertwig & Co.	GM 1883	A,B,C doll heads
	J.D. Kestner jr.	ca 1897	dolly face
151	Hertel, Schwab & Co.	ca 1912	with and without "made in Germany", character, solid dome, painted or sleep eyes, open or open/closed mouth, molded tongue, ill. 632
	Hertel, Schwab & Co.	ca 1912	same as before, but with "2046"
	Simon & Halbig	ca 1912	character, painted eyes, closed mouth, molded teeth, laughing

Mold No.	Firm	Date	Description and Identification
151	Gebr. Ohlhaver	ca 1920	Triangle with sun and eye, character
	C.F. Kling	ca 1885	shoulder head with molded hair and molded blouse, glass eyes, closed mouth, ill. 973
	J.D. Kestner jr.	ca 1897	dolly face
152	Hertel, Schwab & Co.	ca 1912	character, sleep eyes, open mouth, ill. 627
	Hertel, Schwab & Co.	ca 1912	same as before, but with "LW&Co." for Louis Wolf & Co.
	Simon & Halbig	ca 1912	character, painted eyes, closed mouth
	J.D. Kestner jr.	ca 1897	dolly face
153	Simon & Halbig	ca 1912	character, molded hair, painted eyes, closed mouth
	J.D. Kestner jr.	ca 1887	dolly face, solid dome with 2 holes, glass eyes, closed mouth
154	Hertel, Schwab & Co.	ca 1912	character, solid dome, glass eyes, closed mouth, for Kley & Hahn
	J.D. Kestner jr.	ca 1897	shoulder head, dolly face
155	J.D. Kestner jr.	ca 1897	dolly face
156	Simon & Halbig	GM 1926	"AHW", character, for Adolf Hülss
	C.F. Kling	ca 1885	shoulder head, molded hair painted eyes, closed mouth, ill. 974
	J.D. Kestner jr.	GM 1898	dolly face
157	Simon & Halbig	GM 1927	"AHW", character, for Adolf Hülss
	Hertel, Schwab & Co.	ca 1912	character, sleep eyes, closed mouth, ill. 638

Mold No.	Firm	Date	Description and Identification
157	unknown	ca 1900	straight neck, glass eyes, laughing, closed mouth with molded teeth, clown head, **ill. 1265**
158	Hertel, Schwab & Co.	ca 1911	"K&H", character, painted eyes, open mouth, for Kley & Hahn
159	Hertel, Schwab & Co.	GM 1911	multi-face, crying + laughing, also as single heads possibly, crying or laughing, painted eyes and open/closed mouth, for Kley & Hahn, **ill. 953 + 977**
	Simon & Halbig	ca 1911	character
	J.D. Kestner jr.	ca 1898	dolly face, shoulder head
160	Simon & Halbig	ca 1914	"H.H.-S&H", character, sleep eyes, open mouth, for Heinrich Handwerck
	Hertel, Schwab & Co.	ca 1912	"K&H", character, sleep eyes, open/closed mouth, for Kley & Hahn
	C.F. Kling	ca 1885	shoulder head with molded hair and hat, glass eyes, closed mouth, molded blouse
	J.D. Kestner jr.	ca 1898	dolly face
161	Hertel, Schwab & Co.	ca 1912	character, sleep eyes, open/closed mouth, for Kley & Hahn
	J.D. Kestner jr.	ca 1898	dolly face
162	Hertel, Schwab & Co.	ca 1912	character, sleep eyes, open mouth, with cut out for voice, for Kley & Hahn
	J.D. Kestner jr.	ca 1898	dolly face
163	Hertel, Schwab & Co.	ca 1914	character, molded bobbed hair, googly eyes, closed smiling mouth, Jubilee-Doll, for Strobel & Wilken, **ill. 640**

Mold No.	Firm	Date	Description and Identification
163	unknown	ca 1912	character, painted eyes, closed mouth
164	Simon & Halbig	ca 1912	with and without "S&H", glass eyes, open mouth, Oriental
	J.D. Kestner jr.	ca 1898	dolly face
165	Hertel, Schwab & Co.	ca 1914	character, googly eyes, smiling/closed mouth, **ill. 635**
	Gebr. Kühnlenz	ca 1900	"Gbr.K.", dolly face
166	Hertel, Schwab & Co.	ca 1912	"K&H", character, solid, dome, sleep eyes, closed mouth, for Kley & Hahn
	J.D. Kestner jr.	GM 1898	dolly face, shoulder head
167	Hertel, Schwab & Co.	ca 1912	"K&H", character, sleep eyes open/closed or open mouth, for Kley & Hahn
	C.F. Kling	ca 1885	incised bell, shoulder head, solid dome with wig, closed mouth, **ill. color 82**
	J.D. Kestner jr.	ca 1898	dolly face
168	J.D. Kestner jr.	ca 1898	dolly face
169	Hertel, Schwab & Co.	ca 1912	"K&H", character, sleep eyes, with closed or open/closed mouth, for Kley & Hahn, **ill. 927**
	Porzellanfabrik Burggrub	ca 1930	character
	J.D. Kestner jr.	ca 1898	dolly face
170	Kämmer & Reinhardt	GM 1925	newborn, solid dome
	Hertel, Schwab & Co.	ca 1915	"K&H", character, sleep eyes, laughing, open mouth, for König & Wernicke

Mold No.	Firm	Date	Description and Identification
170	Porzellanfabrik Burggrub	ca 1930	"SHPB", character
	Geo. Borgfedlt & Co.	GM 1927	character
	Simon & Halbig	GM 1911	presumably character
	J.D. Kestner jr.	ca 1903	dolly face
171	Kämmer & Reinhardt	GM 1925	Klein-Mammy, newborn
	Simon & Halbig	GM 1911	presumably character
	J.D. Kestner jr.	ca 1900	dolly face, **ill. color 76**
172	Hertel, Schwab & Co.	ca 1914	solid dome, googly eyes, smiling, closed mouth, Jubilee-Doll, for Strobel & Wilken
	Simon & Halbig	GM 1911	presumably character
	J.D. Kestner jr.	ca 1900	shoulder head, glass eyes, closed mouth, Gibson-Girl
	C.F. Kling	ca 1890	dolly face, shoulder head, glass eyes, closed mouth
173	Kämmer & Reinhardt	GM 1925	"K&R S&H", solid dome, newborn, also made with mold number # "8173"
	Hertel, Schwab & Co.	ca 1914	character, solid dome, googly eyes, smiling/closed mouth, Jubilee-Doll, for Strobel & Wilken, **ill. 631**
	Simon & Halbig	GM 1911	presumably character
174	unknown	ca 1912	"LH", character, solid dome, open/closed mouth
	Simon & Halbig	GM 1911	"Superior", character, for Heinrich Handwerck
	J.D. Kestner jr.	ca 1905	dolly face
175	Kämmer & Reinhardt	GM 1928	Klein-Mammy, painted bisque

Mold No.	Firm	Date	Description and Identification
175	Hertel, Schwab & Co.	ca 1914	solid dome, winking with left painted eye, right googly eye, closed laughing mouth, ill. 634
	Hertwig & Co.	GM 1916	head
	Simon & Halbig	GM 1911	presumably character
176	Hertel, Schwab & Co.	ca 1912	character, sleep eyes, open mouth with movable tongue
	Simon & Halbig	ca 1925	"S&H", character, sleep eyes, open mouth
	Karl Beck & Alfred Schulze	ca 1925	character, newborn
	C.F. Kling	ca 1885	shoulder head, china, painted features
177	unknown	ca 1920	character, painted eyes, open/closed mouth
178	Hertel, Schwab & Co.	ca 1915	character, solid dome, molded hair, googly eyes, open mouth, for Kley & Hahn
	C.F. Kling	ca 1885	shoulder head, molded hair, glass eyes, closed mouth
	J.D. Kestner jr.	ca 1909	character, painted eyes, open/closed mouth
179	Hertel, Schwab & Co.	ca 1915	"K&W", character, for Koenig & Wernicke
	Gebr. Knoch	ca 1900	dolly face
	unknown	ca 1925	"Butler", character, googly eyes, closed mouth, ill. 2053
	J.D. Kestner jr.	ca 1909	character, painted or glass eyes, open or open/closed mouth
180	Hertel, Schwab & Co.	ca 1915	"K&W", character, googly eyes, laughing, open/closed mouth, for Kley & Hahn, ill. 952

Mold No.	Firm	Date	Description and Identification
180	J.D. Kestner jr.	ca 1910	character, painted eyes, open/closed mouth or with sleep eyes and fur eyebrows
181	Hertel, Schwab & Co.	ca 1915	character, sleep eyes, open mouth
	Gebr. Knoch	ca 1900	dolly face
	J.D. Kestner jr.	ca 1910	character, painted eyes, open/closed mouth, ill. 871
	unknown	ca 1890	shoulder head, solid dome, glass eyes, closed mouth
182	C.F. Kling	ca 1885	shoulder head, molded hair, painted eyes, closed mouth
	J.D. Kestner jr.	ca 1910	character, painted eyes, closed mouth, ill. 872
183	J.D. Kestner jr.	ca 1910	character, glass eyes, open/closed mouth, ill. 873
	unknown	ca 1890	dolly face, solid dome, glass eyes, closed mouth
184	J.D. Kestner jr.	ca 1910	character, painted or glass eyes, closed mouth
185	Gebr. Knoch	ca 1900	"GKN", dolly face
	F&W. Goebel	ca 1900	"Bebe Elite", dolly face for Max Handwerck
	C.F. Kling	ca 1885	shoulder head, molded hair, painted eyes, closed mouth, ill. 974
	J.D. Kestner jr.	ca 1910	character, painted or glass eyes, open/closed mouth, ill. 874
186	C.F. Kling	ca 1885	shoulder head, molded hair, painted eyes, closed mouth

Mold No.	Firm	Date	Description and Identification
186	J.D. Kestner jr.	ca 1910	character, painted eyes, open/closed mouth
187	J.D. Kestner jr.	ca 1910	character, painted eyes, closed mouth
188	C.F. Kling	ca 1885	shoulder head, molded hair, glass eyes, closed mouth
189	Heinrich Handwerck	ca 1900	dolly face, ill. color 44
	Gebr. Knoch	ca 1900	"GKN", dolly face
	J.D. Kestner jr.	ca 1910	character, glass eyes, closed mouth
	C.F. Kling	ca 1885	shoulder head, china, molded hair, painted features, ill. 977
190	Gebr. Knoch	ca 1900	"GKN", dolly face
	C.F. Kling	ca 1885	shoulder head, molded hair, painted or glass eyes closed mouth
	J.D. Kestner jr.	ca 1910	character, painted eyes, open/closed mouth
191	Kämmer & Reinhardt	ca 1900	with and without "K&R", dolly face, ill. color 69
	Porzellanfabrik Rauenstein	ca 1895	"Alice", dolly face, ill. 1401
192	Kämmer & Reinhardt	ca 1900	with and without "K&R", dolly face with closed or open mouth, ill. color 66 + 68
	Gebr. Knoch	ca 1900	"GKN", dolly face
	J.D. Kestner jr.	GM 1910	presumably character with or without glass eyes
193	Gebr. Knoch	ca 1900	"GKN", dolly face

Mold No.	Firm	Date	Description and Identification
195	J.D. Kestner jr.	ca 1910	shoulder head, fur eyebrows, dolly face
196	J.D. Kestner jr.	ca 1910	fur eyebrows, dolly face
199	Heinrich Handwerck	ca 1900	dolly face
	unknown	ca 1915	"Germany",character,sleep eyes, open mouth
	J.D. Kestner jr.	ca 1910	shoulder head, dolly face
	Gebr. Knoch	ca 1900	"GKN", dolly face
200	Kämmer & Reinhardt	1909	character, shoulder head, painted eyes, open/closed mouth (see mold # 100)
	Armand Marseille	GM 1911	"AM 243", character, googly eyes, closed mouth with molded tongue,ill. 1168
	Catterfelder Puppenfabrik	1910	"CP", character, solid dome, painted eyes, open/closed mouth, ill. 206 + color 26
	Walther & Sohn	ca 1922	"W&S", character, googly eyes, closed mouth
	Gebr. Heubach	ca 1915	"W.u.Z.I.", dolly face, for Wagner & Zetsche
	Hertel, Schwab & Co.	ca 1912	"L.W.&Co", character, shoulder head, solid dome, laughing, for Louis Wolf & Co.
	Max Oscar Arnold	ca 1920	"MOA-Welsch",dolly face, for Welsch & Co.
201	Kämmer & Reinhardt	GM 1909	character, shoulder head, painted eyes, closed mouth, (Peter or Marie), (see mold # 101)
	Catterfelder Puppenfabrik	ca 1910	"CP", character, solid dome, painted eyes, open/closed mouth, ill. 204 + color 24
	Baehr & Proeschild	ca 1888	"DEP", dolly face

Mold No.	Firm	Date	Description and Identification
201	Gebr. Knoch	ca 1900	"GKN", dolly face, also made as Black Doll, ill. 1002
	Schützmeister & Quendt	ca 1920	"SQ", character, Baby
	Fritz Dressel	GM 1926	"Dreso-Puppe"
	unknown	ca 1920	"Gy", character, sleep eyes, open mouth
	J.D. Kestner jr.	ca 1915	shoulder head, celluloid
202	Simon & Halbig	GM 1887	"DEP", multi-face, white and black face, ill. 1672 + 1673
	C.F. Kling	ca 1890	shoulder head, china, molded hair, painted features
	Fritz Dressel	GM 1926	"Dreso-Puppe"
203	Gebr. Knoch	ca 1910	character, shoulder head, painted eyes, closed mouth
	Fritz Dressel	GM 1926	"Dreso-Puppe"
	C.F. Kling	ca 1890	shoulder head, molded hair, glass eyes, closed mouth, ill. 986
	J.D. Kestner jr.	ca 1920	"JDK" with turtle mark, character, sleep eyes, open mouth, celluloid
204	Baehr & Proeschild	ca 1888	dolly face, glass eyes, closed mouth
	Gebr. Knoch	ca 1910	character
	Schützmeister & Quendt	ca 1920	"SQ", character, baby
205	Armand Marseille	ca 1918	"AM", character, baby
	Catterfelder Puppenfabrik	GM 1909	character
	Gebr. Knoch	ca 1910	"GKN", character, shoulder head, painted eyes, open/closed mouth, molded tongue, ill. 1001

Mold No.	Firm	Date	Description and Identification
206	Catterfelder Puppenfabrik	GM 1909	character
	J.D. Kestner jr.	ca 1910	character, sleep eyes, closed mouth
	Gebr. Knoch	ca 1910	"Made in Germany DRGM", character, solid dome, painted eyes, open/closed laughing mouth, Black Doll
207	Baehr & Proeschild	ca 1888	dolly face, glass eyes, closed mouth
	Catterfelder Puppenfabrik	ca 1910	character, painted eyes, closed mouth, **ill. 210 + color 27**
	Adolf Greuling	GM 1897	Harlequin
208	Heinrich Graeser	GM 1891	head
	Catterfelder Puppenfabrik	ca 1910	"CP deponiert", character, with solid dome or wig, painted or sleep eyes, open mouth, movable tongue, **ill. 205 + 209 + color 25**
	Gebr. Knoch	ca 1910	"GKN", character, shoulder head
	Walther & Sohn	ca 1920	"W&S", character, googly eyes, closed mouth, **ill.1900**
	Adolf Greuling	GM 1897	Harlequin
	J.D. Kestner jr.	ca 1910	character, painted or glass eyes, closed mouth
209	Baehr & Proeschild	ca 1888	with and without "Germany", glass eyes, open mouth, dolly face
	Catterfelder Puppenfabrik	ca 1910	"CP", character, sleep eyes, open mouth, movable tongue
	Adolf Greuling	GM 1897	Harlequin
210	Armand Marseille	GM 1911	"AM 243", character, solid head, painted googly eyes, closed mouth, **ill. 1169**

59

Mold No.	Firm	Date	Description and Identification
210	Richard Scherzer	GM 1926	newborn (a 3 day old baby)
	Fritz Dressel	GM 1926	"Dreso-Puppe"
	presumable Theodor Wendt	ca 1925	"T" in "W", character, glass eyes, open mouth
	J.D. Kestner jr.	ca 1912	character, shoulder head, solid dome, sleep eyes, open/closed mouth, **ill. 894**
211	J.D. Kestner jr.	ca 1912	"JDK", character, sleep eyes, open or open/closed mouth, **ill. 892**
	Fritz Dressel	GM 1926	"Dreso-Puppe"
212	Baehr & Proeschild	ca 1888	dolly face, glass eyes, closed mouth
	Fritz Dressel	GM 1926	"Dreso-Puppe"
	J.D. Kestner jr.	ca 1910	"JDK", character, painted or glass eyes, closed mouth, **ill. color 78**
213	Baehr & Proeschild	ca 1888	dolly face
	Hertwig & Co.	GM 1910	presumably character
214	Hertwig & Co.	GM 1910	presumably character
	Kämmer & Reinhardt	GM 1909	character, shoulder head, painted eyes, closed mouth (Hans or Gretchen)(see mold # 114) **ill. 791**
	C.F. Kling	ca 1890	shoulder head, molded hair, glass eyes, closed mouth
	J.D. Kestner jr.	ca 1910	"JDK", with and without fur eyebrows
215	J.D. Kestner jr.	ca 1910	"JDK", with fur eyebrows
216	Gebr. Knoch	ca 1912	"GKN", character, shoulder head, solid dome, painted eyes, laughing, open/closed mouth, **ill. 1000 + 1152**

Mold No.	Firm	Date	Description and Identification
216	C.F. Kling	GM 1881	movable child
	J.D. Kestner jr.	ca 1912	dolly face
217	F&W. Goebel	ca 1900	"WG", dolly face, for Max Handwerck
	Gebr. Knoch	ca 1912	"GKN", character, solid dome, laughing
	C.F. Kling	ca 1885	shoulder head, molded hair, glass eyes, closed mouth
218	Catterfelder Puppenfabrik	ca 1912	character, solid dome, sleep eyes, open mouth with movable tongue
	J.D. Kestner jr.	ca 1912	"JDK", character, solid dome, sleep eyes, open mouth
219	Baehr & Proeschild	ca 1888	dolly face, sleep eyes, open mouth, **ill. color 12**
	Catterfelder Puppenfabrik	ca 1910	character, painted eyes, closed mouth
	Ernst Heubach	ca 1912	character, googly eyes, closed laughing mouth
	J.D. Kestner jr.	GM 1912	presumably character
220	Baehr & Proeschild	ca 1888	dolly face, glass eyes, closed mouth, oriental, **ill. 80**
	Catterfelder Puppenfabrik	ca 1912	"CP", character, sleep eyes, open/closed mouth
	C.F. Kling	ca 1890	incised bell, shoulder head, china, molded hair, painted features
	Fritz Dressel	GM 1926	"Dreso-Puppe"
	J.D. Kestner jr.	ca 1912	"JDK", character, sleep eyes, open/closed mouth
221	J.D. Kestner jr.	ca 1913	"JDK ges.gesch.", character, googly eyes, smiling closed mouth (presumably made after

Mold No.	Firm	Date	Description and Identification
	(see preceding page)		Kewpie-Copyright by Rose O'Neill in 1913), **ill.color 74**
223	Armand Marseille	ca 1913	"AM", character, googly eyes, closed mouth
	Gebr. Knoch	ca 1912	"GKN GES.No.GESCH", character, shoulder head, solid dome, painted eyes, molded tears, closed mouth, **ill. color 84**
	Hermann Steiner	1926	"HS DRGM 954642", character with "living Steiner-eye"
224	Baehr & Proeschild	GM 1888	glass eyes, closed mouth, Red Indian, **ill. 71**
	Theodor Recknagel	ca 1925	character, molded bonnet
225	Baehr & Proeschild	GM 1888	dolly face
	Armand Marseille	ca 1920	"AM", character, sleep eyes, open mouth
	Fritz Dressel	GM 1926	"Dreso-Puppe"
	Kämmer & Reinhardt	ca 1920	shoulder head, celluloid
226	Baehr & Proeschild	GM 1888	dolly face
	Theodor Recknagel	GM 1910	character
	J.D. Kestner jr.	ca 1912	"JDK", character, sleep eyes, open mouth
227	Baehr & Proeschild	GM 1888	dolly face
	Theodor Recknagel	GM 1910	character
230	Baehr & Proeschild	ca 1888	shoulder head, glass eyes, open or closed mouth, dolly face, **ill. color 11**
	Armand Marseille	1912	"AM", with or without "Fany", character, solid dome, sleep eyes, closed mouth, **ill. 1241**

Mold No.	Firm	Date	Description and Identification
230	Gebr. Knoch	ca 1912	"GKN", character, shoulder head, molded bonnet, painted eyes, open/closed laughing mouth
	Fritz Dressel	GM 1926	"Dreso-Puppe"
231	Armand Marseille	GM 1912	"AM 248 Fany", character, sleep eyes, closed mouth, **ill. 1240**
	August Steiner Köppelsdorf	ca 1930	"A.S.", character, baby
232	Gebr. Knoch	ca 1912	"GKN", character, shoulder head, molded bonnet, painted eyes, open/closed laughing mouth
	Theodor Recknagel	ca 1920	character, molded bonnet
	Swaine & Co.	ca 1912	character, solid dome, glass-eyes, open mouth, variation of "Lori" GM 1910 with closed mouth
233	Armand Marseille	ca 1920	with and without "AM", character, sleep eyes, open mouth
234	J.D. Kestner jr.	ca 1914	"JDK", character, shoulder head, solid dome, glass eyes, open/closed mouth
235	Ernst Heubach	ca 1905	dolly face
	J.D. Kestner jr.	ca 1914	"JDK", character, shoulder head, glass eyes, open mouth
236	Ernst Heubach	ca 1905	dolly face
	J.D. Kestner jr.	GM 1913	"JDK", character, sleep eyes, open mouth
237	Ernst Heubach	ca 1905	dolly face
	J.D. Kestner jr.	GM 1914	"JDK GES gesch. 1070 Hilda", character, sleep eyes, open mouth

Mold No.	Firm	Date	Description and Identification
238	Ernst Heubach	ca 1905	dolly face
	unknown	ca 1914	character, solid dome, painted eyes, closed mouth
239	Baehr & Proeschild	ca 1888	dolly face, glass eyes, closed mouth, ill. 79
	J.D. Kestner jr.	ca 1914	"JDK", character, sleep eyes, open mouth
240	Armand Marseille	ca 1914	"AM", character, solid dome, painted googly eyes, closed mouth
	Hermann Steiner	ca 1925	"HS", newborn, sleep eyes, closed mouth
	Fritz Dressel	GM 1926	"Dreso-Puppe"
	unknown	ca 1914	Kewpie type, molded quiff on top, solid dome, googly eyes, closed mouth
	Baby Phyllis Doll Co.	ca 1925	"BABY PHYLLIS Made in Germany", newborn, flange neck, sleep eyes, closed mouth
241	Ernst Heubach	ca 1905	dolly face
	Walther & Sohn	ca 1920	"W&S", shoulder head
	Theodor Recknagel	ca 1925	"LA&S/R&A", newborn, sleep eyes, closed mouth, flange neck, for Louis Amberg & Son
	unknown	ca 1925	"KB", newborn, flange neck, glass eyes, closed mouth
	unknown	ca 1914	Kewpie type, googly eyes, closed mouth
	J.D. Kestner jr.	ca 1914	"JDK", character, sleep eyes, open mouth
242	Armand Marseille	ca 1930	"AM", character, painted bisque
242	Ernst Heubach Hermann Steiner	ca 1930 1926	character, painted bisque "HS DRGM 954642", character with "living Steiner-eye"

Mold No.	Firm	Date	Description and Identification
242	unknown	ca 1925	"KB", newborn, flange neck, glass eyes, closed mouth
	J.D. Kestner jr.	ca 1914	"JDK", character, sleep eyes, open mouth
243	J.D. Kestner jr.	ca 1914	"JDK", character, sleep eyes, open mouth, Oriental, also with all bisque body, ill. 897 + 898 + 899
	unknown	ca 1920	character, solid dome, painted eyes, laughing open/closed mouth, 2 teeth below
244	Baehr & Proeschild	ca 1888	Red Indian
	Armand Marseille	ca 1930	"AM", character, painted bisque
245	Hermann Steiner	ca 1925	"HS", character, baby, glass eyes, closed mouth
	Baehr & Proeschild	ca 1888	dolly face, shoulder head, glass eyes, open mouth
	Kämmer & Reinhardt	ca 1920	shoulder head, celluloid
	J.D. Kestner jr.	GM 1914	"JDK jr. Hilda", character, sleep eyes, open mouth, also as black doll, ill. 895
246	Armand Marseille	ca 1930	character, painted bisque
	Baehr & Proeschild	ca 1888	dolly face, shoulder head
	Hermann Steiner	ca 1920	"HS", character, baby, laughing
	Kämmer & Reinhardt	ca 1920	shoulder head, celluloid
	J.D. Kestner jr.	GM 1915	"JDK", character, sleep eyes, open mouth
247	Baehr & Proeschild	GM 1889	"DEP", dolly face, sleep eyes, open mouth
	C.F. Kling	ca 1890	shoulder head, glass eyes, closed mouth

Mold No.	Firm	Date	Description and Identification
247	Hermann Steiner	ca 1926	"HS DRGM 954642", character with "living Steiner-eye"
	unknown	ca 1925	"KB", newborn, flange neck, glass eyes, closed mouth
	J.D. Kestner jr.	GM 1915	"JDK", character, sleep eyes, open mouth
248	Baehr & Proeschild	GM 1889	dolly face
	Kämmer & Reinhardt	ca 1920	shoulder head, celluloid
249	J.D. Kestner jr.	ca 1915	"JDK", character, sleep eyes, open mouth
250	Baehr & Proeschild	ca 1890	dolly face
	Josef Bergmann	GM 1890	movable dolls
	J.D. Kestner jr.	ca 1920	"JDK", Walküre, dolly face, for Kley & Hahn
	Armand Marseille	GM 1912	"AM DRGM 248 GB", character, solid dome, painted eyes, open mouth, for Geo. Borgfeldt & Co. ill. 1242
	Ernst Heubach	ca 1914	character, with or without pierced nostrils, sleep eyes, open mouth
	Walther & Sohn	ca 1920	"W&S", character, shoulder head
251	Baehr & Proeschild	GM 1889	dolly face
	Armand Marseille	GM 1912	"AM 248", character, baby, for Geo. Borgfeldt & Co.
	Ernst Heubach	ca 1914	character
252	Baehr & Proeschild	GM 1889	"DEP", dolly face, glass eyes, open mouth, ill. color 110 + ill. 1971 + 1972
	Schützmeister & Quendt	ca 1920	"SQ", character, Black Doll
	Ernst Heubach	ca 1914	character, solid dome, sleep eyes, closed mouth, Black Doll

Mold No.	Firm	Date	Description and Identification
252	Armand Marseille	GM 1912	"AM 248", character, solid dome with molded quiff on top, painted eyes, closed mouth
253	Baehr & Proeschild	GM 1889	dolly face
	Armand Marseille	1925	"AM Nobbikid Reg.U.S.Pat. 066 Germany", character, googly eyes, closed mouth, **ill. 1170**
254	Armand Marseille	ca 1912	"AM", character, solid dome, painted eyes, closed mouth
	C.F. Kling	ca 1890	shoulder head, molded hair, painted eyes, closed mouth
	J.D. Kestner jr.	GM 1916	presumably character
255	Armand Marseille	ca 1920	character, solid dome, painted eyes, closed mouth
	Kämmer & Reinhardt	ca 1920	shoulder head, celluloid
	Porzellanfabrik Mengersgereuth	ca 1920	"PM", character, googly eyes, closed mouth, **ill. 1418**
	J.D. Kestner jr.	ca 1916	"O.I.C. made in Germany", character, solid dome, tiny glass eyes, large, open/ closed crying mouth, **ill. 896**
256	Armand Marseille	ca 1920	"AM" with and without "Maar", character, baby, for E.Maar & Sohn
	Kämmer & Reinhardt	ca 1920	shoulder head, celluloid
257	J.D. Kestner jr.	ca 1916	"JDK", character, sleep eyes open mouth
	Armand Marseille	ca 1913	"AM", character, googly eyes, closed mouth
259	Baehr & Proeschild	GM 1890	dolly face

Mold No.	Firm	Date	Description and Identification
259	Armand Marseille	ca 1920	"AM GB", character, baby, for Geo. Borgfeldt & Co.
	Ernst Heubach	ca 1914	character
260	Baehr & Proeschild	GM 1890	"dep", dolly face, glass eyes, closed mouth
	Ernst Heubach	GM 1914	character
	Josef Bergmann	GM 1890	movable doll
	J.D. Kestner jr.	ca 1916	"JDK", character, sleep eyes open mouth
261	Baehr & Proeschild	GM 1890	"DEP", dolly face, glass eyes, closed mouth, ill. 77
	Ernst Heubach	GM 1914	character
	August Steiner Köppelsdorf	ca 1930	"AS", character, compo, also as Black Doll
262	Baehr & Proeschild	GM 1890	dolly face
	Catterfelder Puppenfabrik	ca 1916	character, sleep eyes, open mouth, movable tongue
	Ernst Heubach	GM 1914	"EH", character, painted googly eyes, closed mouth
	J.D. Kestner jr.	ca 1916	"K&Co", character, sleep eyes, open mouth
263	Baehr & Proeschild	GM 1890	dolly face
	Ernst Heubach	GM 1914	character
	J.D. Kestner jr.	ca 1916	"JDK", character, sleep eyes, open mouth, also made for Catterfelder Puppenfabrik
264	Baehr & Proeschild	GM 1890	dolly face
	Ernst Heubach	GM 1914	character
	J.D. Kestner jr.	ca 1916	"K&CO", character, sleep eyes, open mouth, for Catterfelder Puppenfabrik

Mold No.	Firm	Date	Description and Identification
265	Baehr & Proeschild	GM 1890	dolly face
	Rempel & Breitung	ca 1925	"RB/117", dolly face, glass eyes, open mouth
	Kämmer & Reinhardt	ca 1920	shoulder head, celluloid
266	Armand Marseille	ca 1930	"AM", molded braids
	Ernst Heubach	GM 1915	character
267	Ernst Heubach	GM 1914	character
268	Ernst Heubach	GM 1914	character
269	Baehr & Proeschild	ca 1890	"DEP", dolly face
	Ernst Heubach	GM 1914	"EH", character, solid dome, painted eyes, closed mouth
	Franz Schmidt & Co.	ca 1900	"S&C", dolly face
270	Baehr & Proeschild	ca 1890	"DEP", dolly face, shoulder head
	Armand Marseille	ca 1920	"AM", shoulder head
	Catterfelder Puppenfabrik	ca 1920	character
271	Ernst Heubach	GM 1914	"EH", shoulder head, solid dome, painted eyes, closed mouth
	unknown	ca 1915	character, painted googly eyes, smiling, closed mouth
272	J.D. Kestner jr.	ca 1925	"Siegfried made in Germany" newborn, flange neck, sleep eyes, closed mouth
273	Baehr & Proeschild	GM 1891	"DEP", dolly face, sleep eyes, closed mouth
	Armand Marseille	ca 1939	"AM", shoulder head, compo

Mold No.	Firm	Date	Description and Identification
274	Ernst Heubach	GM 1915	character
275	Baehr & Proeschild	GM 1891	dolly face
	Ernst Heubach	ca 1915	shoulder head
	Armand Marseille	ca 1936	"AM", shoulder head, made in painted bisque and compo
276	Armand Marseille	ca 1936	"AM", shoulder head, made in painted bisque and compo
	Ernst Heubach	GM 1915	"EH", character, solid dome, painted eyes, closed mouth with molded bee on top of the nose
277	Baehr & Proeschild	GM 1891	"DEP", dolly face, also made as Black Doll, ill. 78
278	Baehr & Proeschild	GM 1891	"dep", dolly face, shoulder head, sleep eyes, open mouth
279	A. Luge & Co.	GM 1899	doll in stout version
	J.D. Kestner jr.	ca 1925	"Germany CENTURY DOLL & Co" newborn
281	Baehr & Proeschild	GM 1892	dolly face
	Ernst Heubach	GM 1915	character
	J.D. Kestner jr.	ca 1925	"CENTURY DOLL & Co Kestner Germany", newborn, flange neck, sleep eyes, open/closed mouth, ill. 893
282	Ernst Heubach	GM 1915	character
	J.D. Kestner jr.	ca 1920	"Walküre", dolly face, for Kley & Hahn
283	Baehr & Proeschild	GM 1892	dolly face
	Ernst Heubach	GM 1915	"EH", character, molded hair and bow, painted eyes, open/closed mouth

Mold No.	Firm	Date	Description and Identification
283	F&W. Goebel	ca 1900	dolly face, for Max Handwerck
	A. Luge & Co.	GM 1899	doll in stout version
284	Ernst Heubach	GM 1915	character
285	Baehr & Proeschild	GM 1892	dolly face
285	F&W. Goebel	ca 1900	dolly face, for Max Handwerck
	C.F. Kling	ca 1890	shoulder head, molded hair, china, painted features
286	F&W. Goebel	ca 1900	"Bebe Elite", dolly face for Max Handwerck
287	Baehr & Proeschild	GM 1892	dolly face
289	Baehr & Proeschild	GM 1892	"DEP", dolly face, ill. 1955
	Ernst Heubach	ca 1915	"EH", character, molded hair, painted googly eyes, closed mouth with molded, stick out tongue ill. 679 + 685
290	C.F. Kling	ca 1890	incised bell, shoulder head, molded hair, painted eyes, closed mouth
291	Ernst Heubach	ca 1915	"EH", character, glass eyes, closed mouth
292	Baehr & Proeschild	GM 1892	dolly face
	Ernst Heubach	ca 1915	"EH", character, solid dome, sleep eyes, open mouth
	J.D. Kestner jr.	ca 1930	"KH 1930", character, for Kley & Hahn
293	Franz Schmidt & Co.	ca 1900	"S&C", dolly face, ill. 1353

Mold No.	Firm	Date	Description and Identification
293	Carl Knoll, Böhmen	ca 1900	"CK", dolly face, shoulder head, glass eyes, open mouth
297	Baehr & Proeschild	GM 1893	dolly face
300	Ernst Heubach	ca 1920	character, sleep eyes, open mouth
	Armand Marseille	ca 1925	"AM/MH", flapper, glass eyes, closed mouth. ill. 1246
	C.F. Kling	ca 1890	incised bell, shoulder head, molded hair, painted eyes, closed mouth
	Schützmeister & Quendt	ca 1920	"SQ", character, baby
	Oskar Bauer	GM 1926	baby
301	Baehr & Proeschild	GM 1893	dolly face
	Ernst Heubach	ca 1920	dolly face
	Wiefel & Co.	ca 1912	"W&Co", dolly face
	Schützmeister & Quendt	ca 1920	"SQ", character, baby, also found with incised date on crown cutting line: 18.1.21
302	Baehr & Proeschild	GM 1893	dolly face
	Ernst Heubach	ca 1920	dolly face
303	C.F. Kling	GM 1897	soldier head with molded cap, painted eyes, closed mouth, molded mustache
304	Nicole B. Döbrich	GM 1892	dolly face
305	Louis Wolf & Co.	ca 1910	"Germany Queen Louise", dolly face, sleep eyes, open mouth, presumably made by Armand Marseille
	Baehr & Proeschild	GM 1893	dolly face

Mold No.	Firm	Date	Description and Identification
305	C.F. Kling	GM 1897	soldier head with molded cap, painted eyes, closed mouth, molded mustache
	Nicole B. Döbrich	GM 1892	dolly face
306	Baehr & Proeschild	GM 1893	"dep", dolly face
309	Baehr & Proeschild	ca 1893	dolly face, shoulder head, glass eyes, open mouth, ill. 70 + 56
	Armand Marseille	ca 1920	shoulder head
310	Armand Marseille	ca 1929	"AM JUST ME", character, googly eyes, closed mouth, for Geo. Borgfeldt & Co.
312	Ernst Heubach	ca 1922	"SUR", character, for Seyfarth & Reinhardt, ill. 1652
313	Baehr & Proeschild	GM 1893	dolly face
	Ernst Heubach	ca 1922	"SUR", character, for Seyfarth & Reinhardt
317	F&W. Goebel	GM 1913	presumably character
	Ernst Heubach	ca 1920	character
318	Armand Marseille	ca 1930	"AM", character, solid dome sleep eyes, open mouth, Black Doll
	Ernst Heubach	ca 1920	"EH", character, googly eyes, closed mouth
	Albin Heß	GM 1923	character
319	Ernst Heubach	ca 1920	"EH", character, googly eyes, tearful features
	F&W. Goebel	GM 1913	presumably character
	Albin Heß	GM 1923	character

Mold No.	Firm	Date	Description and Identification
320	Baehr & Proeschild	GM 1894	"B&P dep", dolly face
	Armand Marseille	GM 1913	"AM 255", character, solid dome, painted googly eyes, closed mouth, ill. 1174
	Ernst Heubach	ca 1920	character, with pierced nostrils
	F&W. Goebel	GM 1913	presumably character
321	Baehr & Proeschild	GM 1894	dolly face
	Ernst Heubach	ca 1920	character
	F&W. Goebel	GM 1913	presumably character
	Unbekannt	ca 1914	"Ges.gesch.", character, googly eyes
322	Baehr & Proeschild	GM 1894	dolly face
	Armand Marseille	ca 1914	"AM", character, solid dome, painted googly eyes, closed mouth
	Ernst Heubach	ca 1915	character, googly eyes, closed smiling mouth
	F&W. Goebel	GM 1913	presumably character
323	Baehr & Proeschild	GM 1894	dolly face
	Armand Marseille	1914-25	"AM", character, googly eyes, closed mouth, also made in compo, ill. 1171
324	Baehr & Proeschild	GM 1894	dolly face
	Armand Marseille	GM 1913	"AM 255", character, solid dome, painted googly eyes, closed mouth, ill. 1172
325	Baehr & Proeschild	ca 1894	dolly face
	Armand Marseille	ca 1915	character, googly eyes, closed mouth

Mold No.	Firm	Date	Description and Identification
326	Armand Marseille	GM 1913	"AM 259", character, solid dome, glass eyes, open mouth
327	Armand Marseille	GM 1913	"AM 259", character, baby, for Geo. Borgfeldt & Co. ill. 153
328	Armand Marseille	GM 1913	"AM 267", character, baby, for Geo. Borgfeldt & Co.
329	Armand Marseille	GM 1913	"AM 267", character, baby, for Geo. Borgfeldt & Co.
330	Baehr & Proeschild	ca 1894	dolly face
	F&W. Goebel	ca 1900	dolly face
333	Armand Marseille	ca 1925	"AM", character, solid dome, Black or Oriental Doll
334	Ernst Heubach	ca 1924	character, glass eyes, open mouth, Black Doll
	Albin Heß	GM 1927	grotesque doll with roguish-eyes
335	Albin Heß	GM 1928	boudoir doll, soft stuffed, with voice
336	Albin Heß	GM 1928	lady doll
337	Albin Heß	GM 1928	gentleman type
338	Albin Heß	GM 1928	lady doll
339	Ernst Heubach	ca 1925	newborn, character, solid dome, sleep eyes, closed mouth, also made as Black or Oriental doll, ill. color 56 + ill. 680 + 270
340	Baehr & Proeschild	ca 1894	"DEP", dolly face, glass eyes, open mouth

Mold No.	Firm	Date	Description and Identification
340	F&W. Goebel	ca 1900	dolly face
	Ernst Heubach	ca 1925	newborn, solid dome, sleep eyes, closed mouth
	Albin Heß	GM 1928	revue doll
341	Vereinigte Köppelsdorfer Porzellanfabriken	GM 1926	"AM", newborn, flange neck, solid dome, sleep eyes, closed mouth, also a Black Doll or Mulatto, My Dream Baby
341K	Vereinigte Köppelsdorfer Porzellanfabriken	GM 1926	"AM", newborn, socket head solid dome, sleep eyes, closed mouth, My Dream Baby
341Ka	Vereinigte Köppelsdorfer Porzellanfabriken	GM 1926	"AM", newborn, socket head, with wig, sleep eyes, closed mouth, ill. color 92 + 1227 + 1228 + 1229, My Dream Baby
342	Baehr & Proeschild	GM 1895	dolly face
	Vereinigte Köppelsdorfer Porzellanfabriken	GM 1926	head
	Ernst Heubach	ca 1926	"Heubach Köppelsdorf", character, sleep eyes, open mouth, also made as Black Doll, often with pacifer-pull-voice, ill. color 54
	Armand Marseille	ca 1926	"AM", newborn, solid dome, sleep eyes, open/closed mouth
343	Baehr & Proeschild	GM 1895	dolly face
	Vereinigte Köppelsdorfer Porzellanfabriken	GM 1927	head
344	Ernst Heubach	ca 1926	character, sleep eyes, open mouth, Black Doll
345	Vereinigte Köppelsdorfer Porzellanfabriken	GM 1926	head
	Armand Marseille	ca 1926	"AM Germany Kiddiejoy", character

Mold No.	Firm	Date	Description and Identification
348	Baehr & Proeschild	GM 1895	dolly face
	Ernst Heubach	ca 1926	newborn, solid dome, glass eyes, closed mouth
349	Ernst Heubach	ca 1926	newborn, solid dome, sleep eyes, closed mouth, **ill. 681**
350	Baehr & Proeschild	GM 1895	"dep",shoulder head,dolly face
	F&W. Goebel	1893	shoulder head, glass eyes, open mouth, dolly face
	Vereinigte Köppelsdorfer Porzellanfabriken	GM 1926	head
	Ernst Heubach	ca 1926	"Heubach Köppelsdorf", character, sleep eyes, open mouth
	Armand Marseille	ca 1926	"AM", character, sleep eyes, closed mouth
351	Vereinigte Köppelsdorfer Porzellanfabriken	GM 1926	head
	Armand Marseille	ca 1926	"AM", newborn, flange neck, sleep eyes, open mouth, My Dream Baby
351K	Armand Marseille	ca 1926	"AM", newborn, socket head, sleep eyes, open mouth, also made as Black Doll, My Dream Baby
	Kämmer & Reinhardt	ca 1935	"K&RW", character, celluloid, flirting eyes, open mouth
352	Vereinigte Köppelsdorfer Porzellanfabriken	GM 1930	"AM", newborn, solid dome, sleep eyes, open mouth
353	Armand Marseille	ca 1926	"AM", newborn, solid dome, sleep eyes, closed mouth, also made as Black Doll or Oriental, **ill. 392 + color 93**
356	Armand Marseille	ca 1926	"AM", newborn, sleep eyes, closed mouth, Oriental

Mold No.	Firm	Date	Description and Identification
359	Adolf Wislizenus	ca 1923	character
360a	Armand Marseille	GM 1913	"AM 252", character, sleep eyes, open mouth
363	Armand Marseille	ca 1930	"AM", Black Doll, compo
369	Armand Marseille	ca 1938	socket or straight neck, closed mouth, compo
370	C.F. Kling	ca 1900	dolly face, sleep eyes, open mouth
	Armand Marseille	ca 1900	"AM", shoulder head, dolly face (1938 also made in painted bisque and compo)
	Max F. Schelhorn	ca 1912	"SS" incised in shield, character, multi-face, laughing and crying, ill. 1526
371	Armand Marseille	ca 1926	"AM L.A.&S DRGM", character, newborn, solid dome, glass eyes, open mouth, for Louis Amberg & Son
372	C.F. Kling	ca 1900	dolly face
	Armand Marseille	ca 1925	"AM Germany Kiddijoy", character, shoulder head, molded hair, painted eyes, open/closed mouth, laughing with two upper teeth
373	C.F. Kling	ca 1900	dolly face, shoulder head
374	Baehr & Proeschild	GM 1896	dolly face
375	Baehr & Proeschild	GM 1896	dolly face
	Armand Marseille	ca 1925	"AM Germany Kiddijoy", character, shoulder head, molded hair, painted eyes, open/closed mouth, laughing, two upper teeth

Mold No.	Firm	Date	Description and Identification
376	Baehr & Proeschild	GM 1896	dolly face
	Armand Marseille	ca 1905	"AM", shoulder head, dolly face
377	C.F. Kling	ca 1900	incised bell or with incised bell and star, for Kämmer & Reinhardt, shoulder head, dolly face, glass eyes, open mouth
	Armand Marseille	ca 1938	"AM", socket head, boy and girl, compo
378	Baehr & Proeschild	GM 1896	dolly face
	Armand Marseille	ca 1930	"AM", socket head, compo
379	Baehr & Proeschild	GM 1896	"B&P dep", dolly face, socket head, glass eyes, open mouth, ill. 86
380	Baehr & Proeschild	GM 1896	dolly face
381	Baehr & Proeschild	GM 1896	dolly face
382	Armand Marseille	ca 1930	"AM", newborn, solid dome, sleep eyes, open mouth
383	Hertwig & Co.	GM 1910	presumably character
384	Armand Marseille	ca 1905	"AM", socket head, dolly face
	Hertwig & Co.	GM 1910	presumably character
385	Hertwig & Co.	GM 1910	presumably character
386	Hertwig & Co.	GM 1910	presumably character
389	Baehr & Proeschild	GM 1897	dolly face
390	Baehr & Proeschild	GM 1897	dolly face
	Armand Marseille	1900-38	"AM", socket head, dolly face

Mold No.	Firm	Date	Description and Identification
390	Armand Marseille	ca 1909	"AM DRGM 377439 DRGM 374830 DRGM 374831", socket head, with fur eyebrows, ill. 1216 + 1217 + 1218
	unknown	ca 1925	"SWC", character, solid dome, painted eyes, open/closed mouth (mold number also found on all-bisque bodies)
390n	Armand Marseille	GM 1912	"AM 246", socket head, dolly face
391	Armand Marseille	1936	"AM", socket head, dolly face
	unknown	ca 1925	"SWC", character, glass eyes open/closed mouth with tongue (mold number also found on all-bisque bodies)
393	Baehr & Proeschild	GM 1897	dolly face
394	Baehr & Proeschild	ca 1897	"B&P", socket head, dolly face, glass eyes, open mouth
395	Armand Marseille	ca 1925	"AM", character, sleep eyes, open mouth
	Hermann Steiner	ca 1930	"HS", straight neck, revue doll
396	Vereinigte Köppelsdorfer Porzellanfabriken	GM 1930	character, Black Doll
	Ernst Heubach	1930	"EH", newborn, flange neck, glass eyes, closed mouth, Black Doll
	Armand Marseille	ca 1936	"AM", socket or straight neck Mulatto
398	Armand Marseille	ca 1927	"AM", newborn, solid dome, glass eyes, closed mouth, Oriental

Mold No.	Firm	Date	Description and Identification
399	Vereinigte Köppelsdorfer Porzellanfabriken	GM 1930	character, Black Doll
	Ernst Heubach	1930	"Heubach, Köppelsdorf", with or without "DRGM", solid dome, sleep eyes, closed mouth, white or Black Doll, South Sea BABY, for Luge & Co., ill. 683 + 1148 + 1149
	Armand Marseille	1936	"AM", character
400	Vereinigte Köppelsdorfer Porzellanfabriken	GM 1926	"AM 343", character, sleep eyes, closed mouth
	Ernst Heubach	ca 1925	character, baby, painted hair
	Oskar Bauer	GM 1926	socket head, celluloid, soft stuffed leather body
	unknown	ca 1925	"SWC", character, sleep eyes, open mouth, ill. 2057 + 2058
401	Armand Marseille	ca 1926	"AM", character, sleep eyes, closed mouth
	Simon & Halbig	ca 1910	"S&H K&R", glass eyes, open mouth, socket head, for Kämmer & Reinhardt
	Hermann Steiner	ca 1912	"HS", character, shoulder head, solid dome, painted eyes, open/closed mouth, laughing ill. 1793
	Berthold Kühn	GM 1928	newspaper boy
402	Simon & Halbig	ca 1910	"S&H K&R", socket head, glass eyes, open mouth, socket head, for Kämmer & Reinhardt
	Berhold Kühn	GM 1928	golf-boy
403	Simon & Halbig	ca 1910	"S&H K&R", socket head, glass eyes, open mouth, for Kämmer & Reinhardt

Mold No.	Firm	Date	Description and Identification
405	unknown	ca 1920	character, painted eyes, closed mouth
406	Kämmer & Reinhardt	ca 1910	"K&R", with turtle mark, socket head, celluloid, glass eyes, open mouth, ill. 838 + 1478
	Armand Marseille	ca 1920	"AM", Black Doll
	Ernst Heubach	ca 1920	"Heubach Köppelsdorf", Black Doll
407	Carl Bergner	GM 1879	doll dressed in nightie
	Ernst Heubach	ca 1920	"EH", character, sleep eyes open mouth
408	presumable J.D. Kestner jr.	ca 1927	"Germany", shoulder head, glass eyes, closed mouth
409	presumable J.D. Kestner jr.	ca 1927	"Germany", shoulder head, glass eyes, closed mouth
410	presumable Armand Marseille	GM 1913	"Germany", character, sleep eyes, open mouth, with movalbe jaw, for Robert Maser, ill. ill. 1157
411	Armand Marseille	ca 1930	"AM", character, baby, compo
414	Ernst Heubach	ca 1925	newborn, solid dome, sleep eyes, open mouth, Black Doll, ill. 686
	Armand Marseille	1937	"AM", compo
418	Ernst Heubach	ca 1926	character, solid dome, molded hair, glass eyes, open big laughing mouth, Black Doll
420	Heinrich Handwerck	ca 1921	"HH", character

Mold No.	Firm	Date	Description and Identification
421	Albin Peterhänsel	GM 1926	cobbler boy
422	unknown	ca 1900	dolly face, sleep eyes, open mouth
427	Ernst Heubach	ca 1926	character, sleep eyes, open mouth
435	unknown	ca 1925	character, sleep eyes, open mouth
437	Ernst Heubach	ca 1926	character, solid dome, sleep eyes, closed mouth
438	Ernst Heubach	ca 1926	character, sleep eyes, open mouth
439	Ernst Heubach	ca 1926	character, googly eyes, closed mouth
444	Ernst Heubach	ca 1926	character, sleep eyes, closed mouth, Black Doll
	unknown	ca 1905	dolly face
445	Ernst Heubach	ca 1925	character, multi-face, black face laughing, white face crying, ill. color 57 + 59
448	Ernst Heubach	ca 1926	character, Black Doll or Red Indian
449	Armand Marseille	ca 1930	"AM", , painted eyes, closed mouth, compo
450	Simon & Halbig	ca 1890	"Dep", multi face, laughing, crying and sleeping
	Armand Marseille	ca 1938	"AM", , sleep eyes, closed mouth, compo

Mold No.	Firm	Date	Description and Identification
450	Ernst Heubach	ca 1930	glass eyes, closed mouth, compo
451	Ernst Heubach	ca 1928	character, solid dome, glass eyes, open mouth, Black Doll
	Armand Marseille	ca 1936	"AM", sleep eyes, open mouth, Red Indian
452	Ernst Heubach	ca 1928	character, solid dome, glass eyes, open mouth, Gipsy or Oriental
453	Armand Marseille	ca 1936	"AM 453", compo, glass eyes, open mouth, Shirley Temple, or "AM 452H", as before, with molded curls
454	Armand Marseille	ca 1930	compo
457	unknown	ca 1905	dolly face
458	Ernst Heubach	ca 1930	character, Black Doll
	Armand Marseille	ca 1936	character, Red Indian, made in bisque and painted bisque
459	Ernst Heubach	ca 1930	character, solid dome, glass eyes, Black Doll, open mouth with big lower lip
463	Ernst Heubach	ca 1930	character, solid dome, sleep eyes, open mouth, laughing Black Doll, ill. color 55
471	Ernst Heubach	ca 1930	character, sleep eyes, closed mouth
478	unknown	ca 1905	dolly face, sleep eyes, open mouth, ill. 2055

Mold No.	Firm	Date	Description and Identification
480	Ernst Heubach	GM 1928	character, solid dome, South Sea-BABY, for A. Luge & Co.
482	unknown	ca 1926	newborn
486	Christian Hopf	GM 1930	jointed doll, Princess Elizabeth
499	unknown	ca 1900	dolly face, shoulder head
500	Simon & Halbig	GM 1910	presumably character
500	Bruno Schmidt	ca 1905	"BSW" incised heart, glass eyes, open mouth, Oriental
	Armand Marseille	GM 1910	"AM 232", character, solid dome, painted eyes, closed mouth
	Adolf Greuling	GM 1901	clown's head
	Hermann von Berg	GM 1926	"HvB", newborn, flange neck, sleep eyes, open mouth, ill. 174
	Arthur Schoenau	ca 1926	"MB", newborn, sleep eyes, open mouth (MB = My Cherub)
500K	Hermann von Berg	GM 1926	"HvB", newborn, sleep eyes, socket head, open mouth
501	F&W. Goebel	ca 1912	"WG" with crown, character, shoulder head, solid dome, painted eyes, open/closed laughing mouth with teeth, ill. color 38 + 41
	Hermann von Berg	GM 1926	newborn, open mouth
	Guido Knauth	ca 1900	"Knauth", dolly face, glass eyes, open mouth, Black Doll, ill. 995
	Adolf Greuling	GM 1901	clown's head
	Franz Kiesewetter	GM 1912	whistling boy

Mold No.	Firm	Date	Description and Identification
502	Adolf Greuling	GM 1901	clown's head
	Franz Kiesewetter	GM 1912	laughing girl
503	Franz Kiesewetter	GM 1912	laughing boy
	unknown	ca 1880	"TR", dolly face, solid dome with 2 or 3 holes, glass eyes, closed mouth
504	Franz Kiesewetter	GM 1912	girl with googly eyes
	Armand Marseille	ca 1930	"AM", compo
505	Franz Kiesewetter	GM 1913	boy with hat
	Armand Marseille	ca 1938	"AM", sailer head, painted eyes, compo
506	unknown	ca 1880	"TR", dolly face, solid dome with 2 or 3 holes, glass eyes, closed mouth
507	Franz Kiesewetter	GM 1913	boy without hat
509	Franz Kiesewetter	GM 1913	boy with painted googly eyes
510	Franz Kiesewetter	GM 1913	sly fellow with glass googly eyes
	Armand Marseille	ca 1930	"AM", compo
	Erste Steinbacher Porzellanfabrik Gustav Heubach	ca 1926	"GH", character, painted eyes, closed mouth, ill. 1782
	unknown	ca 1880	"HL", dolly face, solid dome with 2 or 3 holes, glass eyes, closed mouth
511	Franz Kiesewetter	GM 1913	sly fellow with painted googly eyes

Mold No.	Firm	Date	Description and Identification
513	Armand Marseille	ca 1920	"AM", sleep eyes, open mouth, Black Doll
	Franz Kiesewetter	GM 1913	crying boy
	unknown	ca 1905	dolly face, sleep eyes, open mouth
514	Franz Kiesewetter	GM 1913	crying girl
	Heber & Co.	ca 1905	"HC", dolly face, glass eyes, open mouth
515	Franz Kiesewetter	GM 1914	crying boy without cap
	Armand Marseille	ca 1930	"AM", compo
516	Franz Kiesewetter	GM 1914	crying girl without bonnet
	Armand Marseille	ca 1930	"AM", compo
517	Franz Kiesewetter	GM 1914	shock-headed Peter
518	Armand Marseille	ca 1938	"AM", solid dome, sleep eyes, open mouth, also made in compo
519	Armand Marseille	ca 1938	"AM", flange neck, compo
520	Armand Marseille	GM 1910	"AM 232", character, solid dome, sleep eyes, open mouth, (1938 in compo)
	Baehr & Proeschild	ca 1910	"K&H", character, painted eyes, closed mouth, for Kley & Hahn
525	Hermann Kiesewetter	GM 1926	head with character eyes
	Baehr & Proeschild	ca 1912	"K&H", character, solid dome, painted eyes, open/closed mouth, for Kley & Hahn
526	Baehr & Proeschild	ca 1912	"K&H", character, painted eyes, closed mouth, for Kley & Hahn

Mold No.	Firm	Date	Description and Identification
527	Carl Bergner	GM 1890	universal-doll
529	Baehr & Proeschild	ca 1912	"B&P" with and without "2025", character, painted eyes, closed mouth, for Bruno Schmidt
530	Simon & Halbig	ca 1910	"S&H", dolly face, sleep eyes, open mouth
531	Baehr & Proeschild	ca 1912	"K&H", character, solid dome, painted eyes, open/closed mouth, for Kley & Hahn
535	Baehr & Proeschild	ca 1912	"B&P" incised heart, character
536	Baehr & Proeschild	ca 1912	character, painted eyes, open/closed mouth, ill. 83
537	Baehr & Proeschild	ca 1912	"BSW" incised heart + "2033" character, sleep eyes, closed mouth, for Bruno Schmidt
539	Baehr & Proeschild	ca 1912	"BSW" incised heart and "2o23", character, solid dome, painted eyes, closed mouth, for Bruno Schmidt
540	Simon & Halbig	ca 1910	"S&H", dolly face, glass eyes, open mouth
	Armand Marseille	ca 1930	"GEO", character, baby, for Gebr. Eckhardt
541	Baehr & Proeschild	ca 1912	"WSK", character, solid dome, painted eyes, open/closed mouth, for Wiesenthal,Schindel & Kallenberg, ill. 1939
	Armand Marseille	ca 1926	"AM", newborn, sleep eyes, closed mouth, Oriental

Mold No.	Firm	Date	Description and Identification
542	Armand Marseille	ca 1926	"AM", newborn, flange neck, sleep eyes, open mouth, bisque or compo
546	Baehr & Proeschild	ca 1912	"K&H", character, glass eyes closed mouth, for Kley & Hahn, ill. 951
549	Baehr & Proeschild	ca 1912	"K&H", character, painted eyes, closed mouth, also made in celluloid, for Kley & Hahn
550	Simon & Halbig	ca 1910	"S&H", dolly face, sleep eyes, open mouth
	Armand Marseille	ca 1926	"AM", character, solid dome, sleep eyes, closed mouth
550a	Armand Marseille	ca 1926	"AM", character, wig, sleep eyes, closed mouth, ill. 1182
551	Armand Marseille	ca 1930	"AM", character, flange neck baby
551K	Armand Marseille	ca 1930	"AM", character, baby
554	Baehr & Proeschild	ca 1912	"K&H", character, glass eyes open/closed mouth, crying voice, for Kley & Hahn
556	Karl Schirmer	GM 1925	head
560	Armand Marseille	GM 1910	"AM 232", character, solid dome, painted eyes, open/closed mouth
560a	Armand Marseille	ca 1926	"AM 232", character, wig, sleep eyes, open mouth, ill. 1230 + 1231

Mold No.	Firm	Date	Description and Identification
563	Baehr & Proeschild	ca 1912	"Schneewittchen" (Snow-White), character, solid dome, sleep eyes, open/closed mouth, for Kley & Hahn
			or
		ca 1912	"Schneeglöckchen" (Snow-drop), character, solid dome, sleep eyes, open or open/closed mouth, for Nöckler & Tittel
567	Baehr & Proeschild	GM 1911	character, multi-face, laughing face: glass eyes, open mouth; crying face: painted eyes, open/closed mouth, for Kley & Hahn
568	Baehr & Proeschild	ca 1912	"K&H", character, solid dome, sleep eyes, smiling, for Kley & Hahn
570	Armand Marseille	GM 1910	"AM 232", presumably character
	Simon & Halbig	ca 1910	"S&H", dolly face
571	Baehr & Proeschild	ca 1912	"K&H", character, solid dome, glass eyes, open/closed mouth, laughing, giant-baby, for Kley & Hahn
573	Ernst Heubach	ca 1928	character, sleep eyes, open/closed mouth, molded teeth
580	Armand Marseille	ca 1930	"AM", character
581	Baehr & Proeschild	ca 1912	character, solid dome, painted eyes, open/closed mouth
582	Baehr & Proeschild	ca 1914	"Germany", character, solid dome, sleep eyes, open/closed mouth with two lower teeth
584	Baehr & Proeschild	ca 1914	character, solid dome, sleep eyes, open/closed mouth, ill. 85

Mold No.	Firm	Date	Description and Identification
585	Baehr & Proeschild	ca 1912	"B&P" incised heart or "B&P" in crossed swords, character, sleep eyes, open mouth
590	Armand Marseille	ca 1926	"AM", character, sleep eyes, open/closed mouth, in compo from 1930 on
592	presumable Baehr & Proeschild	ca 1912	character, sleep eyes, open mouth
599	Armand Marseille	ca 1928	"AM", Japanese
600	Armand Marseille	GM 1910	"AM 234", character, shoulder head, painted eyes, closed mouth, ill. color 85
	Simon & Halbig	ca 1912	"S&H", character, sleep eyes, open mouth
	unknown	ca 1910	shoulder head, glass eyes, open mouth
604	Baehr & Proeschild	ca 1920	with or without "B&P" in crossed swords, character, sleep eyes, open/closed or open mouth, ill. 84
606	unknown	ca 1900	"LM", straight neck
607	Simon & Halbig	ca 1912	"S&H", character, sleep eyes, open mouth
608	unknown	ca 1920	character, googly eyes, closed mouth
610	Simon & Halbig	GM 1915	presumably character
	unknown	ca 1915	character, sleep eyes, open mouth

Mold No.	Firm	Date	Description and Identification
610	unknown	ca 1915	"Germany", character, solid dome, painted eyes, open/ closed mouth, like K&R mold # 100
611	Simon & Halbig	GM 1915	presumably character
612	Simon & Halbig	ca 1915	"S&H/CM Bergmann", character, sleep eyes, open mouth
616	Fritz Bierschenk	GM 1910	"FB", presumably character
	Simon & Halbig	ca 1915	"S&H", character, sleep eyes, open mouth, ill. 1734
619	Baehr & Proeschild	ca 1914	"B&P" in crossed swords, character, solid dome, glass eyes, open mouth
620	Armand Marseille	GM 1910	"AM 234", character
	unknown	ca 1935	"PORO", compo
621	Armand Marseille	GM 1910	"AM 234", character
624	Baehr & Proeschild	ca 1915	"B&P" in crossed swords, character
630	Armand Marseille	GM 1910	"AM 234", character, shoulder head, solid dome, painted eyes, open/closed mouth
	Alt, Beck & Gottschalck	ca 1880	dolly face, glass eyes, open or closed mouth, often found on Jumeau-bodies
632	unknown	ca 1935	"PORO", newborn, compo
639	Alt, Beck & Gottschalck	ca 1880	dolly face, shoulder head, solid dome, glass eyes, closed mouth, ill. 6 + 7

Mold No.	Firm	Date	Description and Identification
640	Baehr & Proeschild	GM 1915	presumably character
640a	Armand Marseille	GM 1910	"AM 640a 234", character, shoulder head, painted eyes, closed mouth
641	Baehr & Proeschild	GM 1915	"B&P" in crossed swords, character, sleep eyes, open mouth with tongue
642	Baehr & Proeschild	GM 1915	presumably character
643	Baehr & Proeschild	GM 1915	presumably character
644	Baehr & Proeschild	GM 1915	presumably character
645	Baehr & Proeschild	GM 1915	presumably character
646	Baehr & Proeschild	GM 1915	presumably character
650	Alfred Heinz	GM 1926	Baby with jointed arms and hands
670	Armand Marseille	ca 1925	"AM", shoulder head
678	Baehr & Proeschild	ca 1920	"B&P" or "2099", character, sleep eyes, open mouth, for Bruno Schmidt
680	Kestner & Comp.	ca 1920	"K&CO K&H", with "266 K&H" character, sleep eyes, open mouth, for Kley & Hahn
686	Baehr & Proeschild	ca 1914	"B&P" incised heart, character, googly eyes, closed mouth, ill. 82
693	Simon & Halbig	ca 1915	"S&H", character

Mold No.	Firm	Date	Description and Identification
693	Alt, Beck & Gottschalck	ca 1880	dolly face, shoulder head, glass eyes, closed mouth
696	Alt, Beck & Gottschalck	ca 1880	shoulder head, molded hair painted eyes, closed mouth
	Armand Marseille	ca 1930	with and without "AM", flange neck, sleep eyes, open mouth
698	Alt, Beck & Gottschalck	ca 1880	shoulder head, glass eyes, open or closed mouth
700	Armand Marseille	ca 1920	"AM", character, sleep eyes, closed mouth
	Kämmer & Reinhardt	ca 1910	character, celluloid, see mold # 100
701	Armand Marseille	ca 1920	"AM", character, sleep eyes, closed mouth
	Carl Knoll	ca 1900	"CK", dolly face, sleep eyes, open mouth, ill. 2027
	Kämmer & Reinhardt	ca 1910	"K&R", character, celluloid see mold # 101
707	Baehr & Proeschild	ca 1915	character, googly eyes, closed mouth
709	Simon & Halbig	ca 1887	dolly face, shoulder head, glass eyes, open mouth
710	Armand Marseille	ca 1920	"AM", Red Indian
711	Armand Marseille	ca 1920	"AM", shoulder head, glass eyes, closed mouth
715	Kämmer & Reinhardt	ca 1912	"K&R", character, celluloid see mold # 115

Mold No.	Firm	Date	Description and Identification
716	Kämmer & Reinhardt	ca 1912	"K&R", character, celluloid see mold # 116
717	Kämmer & Reinhardt	ca 1920	"K&R", character, celluloid see mold # 117
718	Kämmer & Reinhardt	ca 1920	"K&R", character, celluloid see mold # 118
719	Kämmer & Reinhardt	ca 1920	"K&R", character, celluloid see mold # 119
	Simon & Halbig	ca 1886	"SH dep", dolly face, glass eyes, open or closed mouth, often found on Edison-Phonograph-Dolls
720	Kämmer & Reinhardt	ca 1920	"K&R", character, celluloid see mold # 120
	Simon & Halbig	GM 1887	"SH dep", shoulder head, expression of a one to two year old child
721	Kämmer & Reinhadt	ca 1920	"K&R", character, celluloid see mold # 121
725	A. Luge & Co.	1930	South-Sea-BABY
	Carl Bergner	GM 1889	doll
726	Kämmer & Reinhardt	1920-30	"K&R", character, celluloid see mold # 126
727	Kämmer & Reinhardt	GM 1914	"K&R", character, celluloid see mold # 127
728	Kämmer & Reinhardt	GM 1915	"K&R", character, celluloid see mold # 128, ill. 836 + 840
	Simon & Halbig	GM 1888	"S&H", laughing face, glass eyes, open/closed mouth with molded teeth

Mold No.	Firm	Date	Description and Identification
729	Simon & Halbig	GM 1888	"S&H", laughing face, glass eyes, open/closed mouth with molded teeth, also made as Black Doll
730	Kämmer & Reinhardt	ca 1920	"K&R", character, celluloid see mold # 130
738	Simon & Halbig	GM 1888	"S&H", dolly face
739	Simon & Halbig	GM 1888	"S&H", dolly face, glass-eyes, closed or open mouth, also made as Black Doll, ill. 1681
740	Simon & Halbig	GM 1888	"S&H", dolly face, shoulder head, solid dome with one hole, glass eyes, closed mouth
	A. Luge & Co.	GM 1910	character baby
	Arthur Krauß	GM 1926	newborn baby with wig
748	Simon & Halbig	GM 1888	"S&H", dolly face
749	Simon & Halbig	GM 1888	"S&H"; dolly face, glass-eyes, closed or open mouth
750	Simon & Halbig	GM 1888	"S&H", dolly face, shoulder head, glass eyes, open mouth
	Armand Marseille	GM 1913	"AM 258", character
758	Simon & Halbig	GM 1888	"S&H", dolly face
759	Simon & Halbig	GM 1888	"S&H", dolly face, glass-eyes, open mouth, also made as Black Doll
760	Simon & Halbig	GM 1888	"S&H", dolly face, shoulder head

Mold No.	Firm	Date	Description and Identification
760	Armand Marseille	ca 1920	"AM", character
768	Simon & Halbig	GM 1888	"S&H", dolly face
769	Simon & Halbig	GM 1888	"S&H", dolly face, also made as Black Doll
770	Simon & Halbig	GM 1888	"S&H", dolly face, shoulder head
772	Alt, Beck & Gottschalck	ca 1880	shoulder head, molded hair, painted eyes, closed mouth
773	Kämmer & Reinhardt	ca 1925	character, celluloid
776	Kämmer & Reinhardt	ca 1925	character, celluloid, Mulatto
777	Kämmer & Reinhardt	ca 1925	character, celluloid, Japanese
	Rudolf Leschhorn	GM 1928	Charles Lindbergh
778	Simon & Halbig	GM 1888	"S&H", dolly face
784	Alt, Beck & Gottschalck	ca 1880	shoulder head, china, molded hair, painted eyes, closed mouth
790	Armand Marseille	ca 1920	"AM", character
800	Armand Marseille	GM 1910	"AM 234", character, sleep eyes, open or open/closed mouth, also made with head voice
	Porzellanfabrik Mengersgereuth	ca 1926	"PM", newborn
	unknown	ca 1926	"Germany", newborn

Mold No.	Firm	Date	Description and Identification
800	Sonneberger Porzellanfabrik	ca 1948	"SP" incised circle, compo, molded Hair, sleep eyes, open mouth (formerly porcelain manufactory of Armand Marseille)
	Carl Harmus	ca 1905	"Harmus", dolly face
	Kämmer & Reinhardt	ca 1928	character, baby, rubber (see mold # 100)
801	unknown	ca 1926	"Germany"; newborn sleep eyes, closed mouth
802	unknown	ca 1900	"W", dolly face
806	unknown	ca 1880	"TR", dolly face, solid dome with three holes, glass eyes, closed mouth, ill. 2035
810	Armand Marseille	ca 1915	"AM", shoulder head, sleep eyes, open/closed mouth
813	unknown	ca 1880	"TR", dolly face, solid dome with three holes, glass eyes, closed mouth
814	unknown	ca 1926	"Germany", character, sleep eyes, open mouth
817	Kämmer & Reinhardt	ca 1928	"K&R", character, rubber (see mold # 117)
820	Armand Marseille	ca 1915	"AM", character, shoulder head, sleep eyes, open/closed mouth, ill. color 88 + 89
826	Kämmer & Reinhardt	ca 1928	"K&R", character, rubber (see mold # 126)
828	Kämmer & Reinhardt	ca 1928	"K&R", character, rubber (see mold # 128)

Mold No.	Firm	Date	Description and Identification
828	Porzellanfabrik Mengersgereuth	ca 1920	"PM", character, molded hair with bow and flowers, painted eyes, open/closed mouth, molded teeth
830	Porzellanfabrik Mengersgereuth	ca 1920	"PM", character
831	Kämmer & Reinhardt	ca 1928	"K&R", character, rubber (see mold # 131)
837	Simon & Halbig	ca 1880	"S&H", dolly face, for all bisque doll
842	unknown	ca 1926	"J.L.Kallus:Copr.Germany", character, solid dome, glass eyes, open mouth, all bisque body, Baby Bo Kaye
845	Simon & Halbig	GM 1878	bathing doll (all-bisque)
846	Simon & Halbig	GM 1878	bathing doll (all-bisque)
847	Simon & Halbig	GM 1880	bathing doll (all-bisque)
848	Simon & Halbig	GM 1880	bathing doll (all-bisque)
852	Simon & Halbig	ca 1880	"S&H", dolly face, for all-bisque doll
866	Alt, Beck & Gottschalck	GM 1895	head
867	Alt, Beck & Gottschalck	GM 1895	head
868	Alt, Beck & Gottschalck	GM 1895	head

Mold No.	Firm	Date	Description and Identification
869	Alt, Beck & Gottschalck	GM 1895	head
870	Alt, Beck & Gottschalck	GM 1895	shoulder head, solid dome, glass eyes, closed mouth
871	Heinrich Bätz	GM 1930	character
873	Kämmer & Reinhardt	ca 1928	"K&R", character, rubber (see mold # 173)
878	Simon & Halbig	ca 1880	"S&H", dolly face, for all-bisque body
879	Alt, Beck & Gottschalck	ca 1895	shoulder head, sleep eyes, closed mouth
880	Simon & Halbig	ca 1880	"S&H", dolly face, for all-bisque doll
	Alt, Beck & Gottschalck	ca 1890	shoulder head, molded hair
881	Simon & Halbig	ca 1880	"S&H", dolly face, for all-bisque doll
882	Dornheim, Koch & Fischer	GM 1892	crossed swords, shoulder head, molded hair, painted features
886	Simon & Halbig	ca 1880	"S&H", dolly face, for all-bisque doll, ill. 1671
	Theodor Recknagel	GM 1926	"AR Germany LA&S", newborn, glass eyes, closed or open mouth
887	Simon & Halbig	ca 1880	"S&H", dolly face, for all-bisque doll
888	Geo. Borgfeldt & Co.	GM 1927	character

Mold No.	Firm	Date	Description and Identification
889	Geo. Borgfeldt & Co.	GM 1927	character
890	Alt, Beck & Gottschalck	ca 1890	shoulder head, molded hair, painted blond or black, painted eyes, closed mouth
	Simon & Halbig	ca 1880	"S&H", dolly face, for all-bisque doll
	Ernst Metzler	ca 1920	"EM", dolly face
890a	Otto Jäger	ca 1922	character
894	Alt, Beck & Gottschalck	ca 1880	shoulder head with molded blue scarf, painted or glass eyes, closed mouth, also found without mold number, **ill. 8**
896	Simon & Halbig	GM 1913	bathing doll with painted or glass sleep eyes
898	Simon & Halbig	GM 1913	bathing doll with painted eyes, stationary glass or sleep eyes
899	Simon & Halbig	GM 1913	bathing doll with painted, stationary or movable glass eyes, (presumably marked with "dep", all-bisque with Moritz features)
900	Armand Marseille	ca 1920	"AM", character
	Porzellanfabrik Burggrub	ca 1930	character, baby
	Kämmer & Reinhardt	ca 1930	"K&R", character, compo (see mold # 100)
	unknown	ca 1880	"TR", shoulder head, solid dome with one hole, glass eyes, closed mouth

Mold No.	Firm	Date	Description and Identification
901	Simon & Halbig	GM 1913	bathing doll with stationary head and arms, or with movable head and arms
	Kämmer & Reinhardt	ca 1930	"K&R", character, compo (see mold # 101)
904	Porzellanfabrik Mengersgereuth	ca 1920	"PM", character
905	Simon & Halbig	ca 1888	"S&H", dolly face, socket or swivel-head, glass eyes, closed mouth, ill. 1676
908	Simon & Halbig	ca 1888	"S&H", dolly face, sleep eyes, open or closed mouth, ill. color 128 + ill. 1677
	unknown	ca 1880	"TR", dolly face, shoulder head, solid dome, glass eyes, closed mouth
909	Simon & Halbig	ca 1888	"S&H", dolly face, glass eyes, open mouth
911	Alt, Beck & Gottschalck	ca 1890	swivel head on shoulder plate, glass eyes, closed mouth
914	Schoenau & Hoffmeister	ca 1925	"SPBH", character
	Porzellanfabrik Mengersgereuth	ca 1920	"PM", character
915	Alt, Beck & Gottschalck	ca 1890	shoulder head, glass eyes, closed mouth
916	Porzellanfabrik Mengersgereuth	ca 1920	"PM", character
917	Kämmer & Reinhardt	ca 1930	"K&R", character, compo (see mold # 117)

Mold No.	Firm	Date	Description and Identification
918	Simon & Halbig	ca 1880	"S&H/K&R", dolly face, for all-bisque doll body marked # "918"
919	Simon & Halbig	ca 1888	"S&H", dolly face, glass eyes, closed mouth with white space
920	Simon & Halbig	ca 1888	"S&H", shoulder head, glass eyes, closed mouth with white space, ill. color 125 + 126
	Armand Marseille	ca 1920	"AM", shoulder head, sleep eyes, open mouth
921	Kämmer & Reinhardt	ca 1930	"K&R", character, compo, (see mold # 121)
	Simon & Halbig	ca 1913	"S&H", character, baby, all-bisque (10 cm = 4 inch.)
924	Porzellanfabrik Mengersgereuth	ca 1920	"PM", character, sleep eyes, open mouth
925	unknown	ca 1900	straight neck, solid dome, painted eyes, open/closed laughing mouth (presumably for automata)
926	Porzellanfabrik Mengersgereuth	GM 1926	character, for Robert Carl
	Kämmer & Reinhardt	ca 1930	"K&R", character, compo (see mold # 126)
927	Porzellanfabrik Mengersgereuth	GM 1926	character, for Robert Carl
	Armand Marseille	ca 1920	"AM", character, baby
	Simon & Halbig	ca 1913	"S&C/S&H", character, for Franz Schmidt & Co., also made only with "S&H"

Mold No.	Firm	Date	Description and Identification
928	Porzellanfabrik Mengersgereuth	ca 1926	"PM", character, molded hair with bow, painted features, for Robert Carl
929	Porzellanfabrik Mengersgereuth	GM 1926	character, for Robert Carl
	Simon & Halbig	ca 1888	"S&H", dolly face, glass eyes, open or closed mouth, also made for all-bisque doll
939	Simon & Halbig	ca 1888	"S&H", dolly face, glass eyes, open or closed mouth, ill. 1674 + 1675
940	Simon & Halbig	ca 1888	"S&H", dolly face, shoulder head, glass eyes, closed mouth, ill. 1678
941	Simon & Halbig	ca 1888	"S&H", shoulder plate, found with "S&H" heads, mold # 939 + 949
949	Simon & Halbig	ca 1888	"S&H", dolly face, glass eyes, open or closed mouth, also made as Black Doll
950	Simon & Halbig	ca 1888	"S&H", dolly face, shoulder head, glass eyes, closed mouth
	Porzellanfabrik Mengersgereuth	ca 1926	"PM", character, googly eyes, closed mouth, ill. 1419
	Armand Marseille	ca 1920	"AM", character, solid dome, painted eyes, closed mouth, ill. 1173
951	Armand Marseille	ca 1920	"AM", character, baby
952	Kämmer & Reinhardt	ca 1930	"K&R", character, compo, Black Doll

Mold No.	Firm	Date	Description and Identification
959	Simon & Halbig	ca 1888	"S&H", dolly face, glass eyes, open mouth
966	Armand Marseille	1938	"AM", character, sleep eyes, open mouth, compo
	Hugo Wiegand	GM 1911	baby
967	Hugo Wiegand	GM 1911	baby
968	Simon & Halbig	GM 1887	"S&H", dolly face, glass eyes, smiling, open mouth
969	Simon & Halbig	GM 1887	"S&H", dolly face, glass eyes, smiling, open mouth, also made as Black Doll
970	Simon & Halbig	GM 1887	"S&H", dolly face, shoulder head, glass eyes, smiling open mouth, also made as Black Doll
	Armand Marseille	ca 1922	"AM", character, also made for Otto Gans
971	Armand Marseille	GM 1913	"AM" with or without "267", character, sleep eyes, open mouth
971a	Armand Marseille	GM 1913	"AM 267", character, also made with voice, ill. 1232
972	Armand Marseille	GM 1926	"AM/LA&S", character, sleep eyes, closed mouth, for Louis Amberg & Son
973	Armand Marseille	GM 1926	"AM/LA&S", character, sleep eyes, closed mouth, for Louis Amberg & Son
	Kämmer & Reinhardt	ca 1930	"K&R", newborn, compo (see mold # 173)

Mold No.	Firm	Date	Description and Identification
974	Alt, Beck & Gottschalck	ca 1890	shoulder head, molded curls, painted eyes, closed mouth
975	Armand Marseille	ca 1922	"AM", character, baby, for Otto Gans
977	Kämmer & Reinhardt	ca 1930	"K&R", compo, Japanese
979	Simon & Halbig	GM 1887	"S&H", dolly face, ill. 1685
980	Armand Marseille	ca 1920	"AM", character, glass eyes, open mouth
982	Armand Marseille	ca 1924	"LA&SNY", character, Baby Peggy Montgomery
984	Armand Marseille	ca 1925	"AM", character, baby
985	Armand Marseille	ca 1925	"AM", character, baby, sleep eyes, open mouth
988	Simon & Halbig	GM 1887	"S&H", dolly face
989	Simon & Halbig	GM 1887	"S&H", dolly face, glass eyes, closed mouth, ill. color 129
990	Simon & Halbig	GM 1887	"S&H", dolly face, shoulder head
	Armand Marseille	ca 1925	"AM", character, baby, also made as Black Doll
991	Vereinigte Köppelsdorfer Porzellanfabriken	GM 1930	"AM", character, sleep eyes, open mouth
992	Armand Marseille	ca 1930	"AM", character, Our Pet, for Gebr. Eckardt
993	Armand Marseille	ca 1925	"AM JIO c 1926", character flange neck, sleep eyes, open mouth, Kiddiejoy

Mold No.	Firm	Date	Description and Identification
995	Armand Marseille	ca 1930	"AM", character, also made as Black Doll, painted bisque or "AM SUR", character, for Seyfarth & Reinhardt
	Hugo Wiegand	ca 1913	character
996	Armand Marseille	ca 1931	"AM", character, baby, painted bisque
997	Armand Marseille	ca 1925	"AM", character, Kiddiejoy
1000	Simon & Halbig	GM 1887	"S&H", dolly face, swivel head
	Alt, Beck & Gottschalck	ca 1890	shoulder head, china or bisque, molded hair, blond or black painted features
	Hermann Steiner	ca 1925	"HS", character
	unknown	ca 1890	dolly face, sleep eyes, open mouth, also made as Black Doll
1001	Wagner & Zetsche	GM 1915	head
	Fritz Lutz	GM 1926	head
1002	Fritz Lutz	GM 1926	head
	Alt, Beck & Gottschalck	ca 1890	shoulder head, molded hair, painted eyes, closed mouth
1003	Fritz Lutz	GM 1926	head
1004	Fritz Lutz	GM 1926	head
1005	Geo. Borgfeldt & Co.	GM 1929	"1420", character, Bonnie Babe
1007	Fritz Lutz	GM 1926	head

Mold No.	Firm	Date	Description and Identification
1008	Simon & Halbig	GM 1889	"S&H", dolly face
	Alt, Beck & Gottschalck	ca 1890	shoulder head, china, molded hair, painted features
1009	Simon & Halbig	GM 1889	"S&H", dolly face, glass eyes, open or closed mouth, also made as Black Doll
1010	Simon & Halbig	GM 1889	"S&H", dolly face, shoulder head, glass eyes, open mouth, ill. 1683
1015	Oskar Schlesinger	GM 1902	doll
1018	Simon & Halbig	GM 1890	"S&H", laughing face
1019	Simon & Halbig	GM 1890	"S&H", laughing face, often found on "Ondine" mechanical swimming doll
1020	Simon & Halbig	GM 1890	"S&H", laughing face, shoulder head
	Alt, Beck & Gottschalck	ca 1890	shoulder head, molded hair with string of pearls, painted eyes, closed mouth
	Oskar Schlesinger	GM 1902	doll
1024	Alt, Beck & Gottschalck	ca 1890	shoulder head
1025	Oskar Schlesinger	GM 1902	doll
1026	Alt, Beck	ca 1890	shoulder head, molded bonnet, painted eyes, closed mouth
1028	Alt, Beck & Gottschalck	ca 1890	shoulder head, molded hair, painted eyes, closed mouth, ill. 4

Mold No.	Firm	Date	Description and Identification
1029	Simon & Halbig	ca 1890	"S&H DRP 56562", dolly face, sleep eye mechanism, open mouth, ill. 1662 + 1663 + 1664
1030	Oskar Schlesinger	GM 1902	doll
1035	Oskar Schlesinger	GM 1902	doll
1038	Simon & Halbig	GM 1891	"S&H", dolly face, glass eyes, open mouth
1039	Simon & Halbig	GM 1891	"S&H", dolly face, sleep eyes, open mouth, also made as Black Doll, (often stamped with "Wimpern geschützt", ill. 1680)
1040	Simon & Halbig	GM 1891	"S&H", dolly face, shoulder head, sleep eyes, open mouth
	Oskar Schlesinger	GM 1902	doll
1041	Simon & Halbig	GM 1891	"S&H", shoulder plate, found with "S&H" socket heads, mold number 939 or 1009 order 1079
1044	Alt, Beck & Gottschalck	ca 1890	shoulder head, painted or glass eyes, closed mouth, ill. 3
1046	Alt, Beck & Gottschalck	ca 1890	shoulder head, molded hiar, glass eyes, closed mouth
	Louis Reber	ca 1924	"DRGM 897388", rubber socket head, painted eyes, open/closed mouth, ill. 1437
1049	Simon & Halbig	ca 1891	"S&H", dolly face, glass eyes, open mouth
1056	Alt, Beck & Gottschalck	ca 1890	shoulder head, molded hair, painted eyes, closed mouth, model Empress Augusta

Mold No.	Firm	Date	Description and Identification
1058	Simon & Halbig	GM 1891	"S&H", dolly face
1059	Simon & Halbig	GM 1891	"S&H", dolly face, glass eyes, open mouth
1060	Simon & Halbig	GM 1891	"S&H", dolly face, shoulder head
1061	Simon & Halbig	GM 1891	"S&H", shoulder plate, ill.271
1064	Alt, Beck & Gottschalck	ca 1890	shoulder head, molded hair, painted eyes, closed mouth, ill. 18
1068	Simon & Halbig	GM 1892	"S&H", dolly face
1069	Simon & Halbig	GM 1892	"S&H", dolly face
1070	Simon & Halbig	GM 1892	"S&H",dolly face,shoulder head
	Koenig & Wernicke	ca 1915	"K&W", character, sleep eyes, open mouth, ill. 1028
1078	Simon & Halbig	GM 1892	"S&H", dolly face, glass eyes, open mouth
1079	Simon & Halbig	GM 1892	"S&H", dolly face, sleep eyes, open mouth, ill. 1952 + 1953 + 1954
1080	Simon & Halbig	GM 1892	"S&H", dolly face, shoulder head
1086	Alt, Beck & Gottschalck	ca 1890	shoulder head, molded blond or black hair, painted eyes, closed mouth, china or bisque with glass eyes
1092	Alt, Beck & Gottschalck	ca 1890	shoulder head, molded hair, painted eyes, closed mouth, model Empress Augusta

Mold No.	Firm	Date	Description and Identification
1098	Simon & Halbig	GM 1893	"S&H", dolly face, Chinese
1099	Simon & Halbig	GM 1893	"S&H", dolly face, Chinese
1100	Catterfelder Puppenfabrik	ca 1908	dolly face, sleep eyes, open mouth, ill. 207
1108	Simon & Halbig	GM 1893	"S&H", dolly face
1109	Simon & Halbig	GM 1893	"S&H", dolly face
1110	Simon & Halbig	GM 1893	"S&H", dolly face, shoulder head
1121	Alt, Beck & Gottschalck	ca 1890	shoulder head, solid dome, glass eyes, closed mouth
1123	Alt, Beck & Gottschalck	ca 1893	"made in Germany", shoulder head, glass eyes, open mouth
1129	Simon & Halbig	ca 1893	"S&H", dolly face, Oriental
1139	Simon & Halbig	ca 1893	"S&H", lady doll
1142	Alt, Beck & Gottschalck	ca 1890	shoulder head, china molded hair, painted eyes, closed mouth
1148	Simon & Halbig	GM 1894	"S&H", dolly face
1149	Simon & Halbig	GM 1894	"S&H", dolly face
1150	Simon & Halbig	GM 1894	"S&H", dolly face, shoulder head
1152	Alt, Beck Gottschalck	GM 1885	"dep", dolly face, glass eyes, open mouth

Mold No.	Firm	Date	Description and Identification
1153	Alt, Beck & Gottschalck	GM 1885	head
1158	Simon & Halbig	GM 1894	"S&H", dolly face
1159	Simon & Halbig	GM 1894	"S&H", dolly face, glass eyes, open mouth, Gibson Girl
1160	Simon & Halbig	GM 1894	"S&H", dolly face, shoulder head, glass eyes, closed mouth, Little Woman, ill. 1682
1170	Simon & Halbig	ca 1895	"S&H", dolly face, shoulder head, glass eyes, open mouth
	Alt, Beck & Gottschalck	GM 1888	head
1171	Alt, Beck & Gottschalck	GM 1888	head
1172	Alt, Beck & Gottschalck	GM 1888	head
1173	Alt, Beck & Gottschalck	GM 1888	head
1174	Alt, Beck & Gottschalck	GM 1888	head
1175	Alt, Beck & Gottschalck	GM 1888	head
1176	Alt, Beck & Gottschalck	GM 1888	head
1177	Alt, Beck & Gottschalck	GM 1888	head

Mold No.	Firm	Date	Description and Identification
1180	Simon & Halbig	ca 1898	"S&H/S&C", dolly face, shoulder head, sleep eyes, open mouth, for Franz Schmidt & Co.
	Heinrich Graeser	GM 1890	jointed bisque doll
1199	Simon & Halbig	ca 1898	"S&H", dolly face, glass eyes, open mouth, Oriental
1200	Catterfelder Puppenfabrik	ca 1908	dolly face, sleep eyes open mouth
	unknown	ca 1900	"MS", dolly face
1210	Alt, Beck & Gottschalck	ca 1890	shoulder head, molded hair, glass eyes, closed mouth
1222	Alt, Beck & Gottschalck	ca 1890	shoulder head, molded hair, painted eyes, closed mouth, **ill. 2**
1226	Bruno Schmidt	GM 1926	head, celluloid, molded bobbed hair, painted eyes
1228	Geo. Borgfeldt & Co.	GM 1902	humorous doll group
1234	Alt, Beck & Gottschalck	GM 1899	dolly face
1235	Alt, Beck & Gottschalck	GM 1899	"DEP", dolly face, shoulder head, glass eyes, open mouth
1236	Alt, Beck & Gottschalck	GM 1899	dolly face
1237	Alt, Beck & Gottschalck	GM 1899	dolly face
1246	Simon & Halbig	ca 1898	"S&H", dolly face

Mold No.	Firm	Date	Description and Identification
1248	Simon & Halbig	GM 1898	"S&H", dolly face, also made as Black Doll
1249	Simon & Halbig	GM 1898	"S&H", dolly face with and without "Santa", for Hamburger & Co.
1250	Simon & Halbig	GM 1898	"S&H", dolly face, shoulder head
	Franz Schmidt & Co.	ca 1902	"FS&C" or "S&C", dolly face, sleep eyes, open mouth, **ill. color 112**
	Alt, Beck & Gottschalck	ca 1899	dolly face
1253	Franz Schmidt & Co.	ca 1902	dolly face
1254	Alt, Beck & Gottschalck	ca 1899	dolly face, shoulder head, molded hair, glass eyes, closed mouth, **ill. 18**
1259	Franz Schmidt & Co.	ca 1912	"FS&Co", character, sleep eyes, pierced nostrils, open mouth
1260	Simon & Halbig	ca 1899	"S&H", dolly face, shoulder head
	Alt, Beck & Gottschalck	GM 1892	"Germany dep", dolly face, shoulder head, glass eyes, open mouth
1261	Alt, Beck & Gottschalck	GM 1892	head
1262	Franz Schmidt & Co.	ca 1912	"FS&Co", character, painted eyes, closed mouth
1263	Franz Schmidt & Co.	ca 1912	"FS&Co", character, painted eyes, closed mouth

Mold No.	Firm	Date	Description and Identification
1266	Franz Schmidt & Co.	ca 1912	"FS&Co", character, solid dome, painted eyes, closed mouth, **ill. 1596**
1267	Franz Schmidt & Co.	ca 1912	"FS&Co", character, solid dome, painted eyes, closed mouth, **ill. 1595**
1268	Alt, Beck & Gottschalck	GM 1892	"Germany Dep.No", dolly face, glass eyes, open mouth, **ill. 10**
1269	Simon & Halbig	ca 1899	"S&H", dolly face
	Alt, Beck & Gottschalck	GM 1892	head
1270	Alt, Beck & Gottschalck	GM 1892	head
	Franz Schmidt & Co.	GM 1910	character
1271	Alt, Beck & Gottschalck	GM 1892	head
	Franz Schmidt & Co.	GM 1910	"FS&Co.Deponiert", character, sleep eyes, closed mouth
1272	Franz Schmidt & Co.	GM 1910	"FS&Co.Deponiert", solid dome or cut out for wig, sleep eyes, pierced nostrils open mouth, movable tongue
1274	Franz Schmidt & Co.	GM 1911	character
1278	Alt, Beck & Gottschalck	GM 1892	head
	Simon & Halbig	GM 1899	"S&H", dolly face, sleep eyes, open mouth
1279	Alt, Beck & Gottschalck	GM 1892	head

Mold No.	Firm	Date	Description and Identification
1279	Simon & Halbig	GM 1899	"S&H", dolly face, sleep eyes, open mouth
1280	Simon & Halbig	GM 1899	"S&H", with and without "Columbia", dolly face, shoulder head, for C.M. Bergmann
1289	Simon & Halbig	GM 1901	head
1290	Alt, Beck & Gottschalck	GM 1893	"made in Germany dep", dolly face, shoulder head, glass eyes, open mouth, ill. 9
1291	Alt, Beck & Gottschalck	GM 1893	head
1293	Simon & Halbig	ca 1912	"FS&Co", character, for Franz Schmidt & Co.
1294	Simon & Halbig	ca 1912	"S&H", character, Baby, also made as Black Doll
1295	Simon & Halbig	ca 1912	"FS&Co" or "S&H", character, sleep eyes, pierced nostrils, open mouth, for Franz Schmidt & Co.
1296	Simon & Halbig	ca 1912	"FS&Co", character, sleep eyes, pierced nostrils, open mouth, open mouth, for Franz Schmidt & Co. or "PO", compo, same as before ca 1930
1297	Simon & Halbig	ca 1912	"FS&Co", character, solid dome, sleep eyes, pierced nostrils, open mouth, movable tongue, for Franz Schmidt & Co.
1298	Simon & Halbig	ca 1912	"FS&Co", character, for Franz Schmidt & Co.

Mold No.	Firm	Date	Description and Identification
1299	Simon & Halbig	ca 1912	"FS&Co" or "S&H", character, for Franz Schmidt & Co.
1300	Simon & Halbig	ca 1902	"S&H DEP", dolly face, glass eyes with eye lashes of thread, open mouth, often found on French automata
1301	Simon & Halbig	ca 1902	"S&H DEP", dolly face, glass eyes with eye lashes of thread, closed mouth, Black Doll
1302	Simon & Halbig	ca 1902	"S&H DEP", dolly face, glass eyes, closed mouth, Black Doll
1303	Simon & Halbig	ca 1902	"S&H DEP", expressive lady face, glass eyes, eye lashes of thread, closed mouth, ill. 1684 or "S&H", expressive Red Indian face, painted eyes, closed mouth, coloured bisque
1304	Simon & Halbig	ca 1902	"S&H", expressive face, glass eyes, closed mouth
1305	Simon & Halbig	ca 1902	"S&H", expressive face, glass-eyes, long nose, open/closed laughing mouth
1307	Simon & Halbig	ca 1902	lady face, glass eyes, eye lashes of thread, closed mouth
1308	Simon & Halbig	ca 1902	"S&H E", dolly face, glass eyes, closed mouth or "S&H D", man, glass eyes, closed mouth, dirty coloured face (charcoal burner), ill. color 124 or "S&H D", man, glass eyes,

Mold No.	Firm	Date	Description and Identification
1308	Simon & Halbig (see page 91)		closed mouth with molded teeth and molded mustache or "S&H D", solid dome, glass eyes, closed mouth, man
1310	Simon & Halbig	ca 1905	"S&C Simon & Halbig", dolly face, for Franz Schmidt & Co. or "FS&C Simon & Halbig", dolly face, for Franz Schmidt & Co.
1321	Alt, Beck & Gottschalck	ca 1910	"ABG", character, solid dome, painted eyes, open/closed mouth or "WSK", same as before, for Wiesenthal, Schindel & Kallenberg
1322	Alt, Beck & Gottschalck	GM 1910	"AB&G" with or without "DRGM", character, solid dome, painted or sleep eyes, open/closed mouth or cut out for wig, sleep eyes, open mouth with movable tongue, ill. 20
1326	Alt, Beck & Gottschalck	1912	"DRGM 520942", character, sleep eyes, open mouth, ill. 17
1329	Simon & Halbig	ca 1910	"S&H", dolly face, Oriental
1339	Simon & Halbig	ca 1908	"S&H L.L.&S", dolly face, sleep eyes, open mouth, ill. 1918
1340	Simon & Halbig	ca 1912	"S&H", character, googly eyes, closed mouth
1342	Alt, Beck & Gottschalck	ca 1912	"ABG", character, sleep eyes, open mouth

Mold No.	Firm	Date	Description and Identification
1348	Simon & Halbig	ca 1910	"S&H Dressel", dolly face, "Jutta", for Cuno & Otto Dressel
1349	Simon & Halbig	ca 1910	"S&H Dressel", dolly face, "Jutta", also made as Black Doll, for Cuno & Otto Dressel, ill. 1982
1351	Simon & Halbig	ca 1913	"HWW", character, for Hugo Wiegand
1352	Alt, Beck & Gottschalck	ca 1912	character, sleep eyes, open mouth
1357	Alt, Beck & Gottschalck	ca 1912	"ABG", character, solid dome, or with wig, painted eyes, open mouth
1358	Simon & Halbig	ca 1910	"S&H", dolly face, glass eyes, open mouth, Black Doll
	Alt, Beck & Gottschalck	ca 1912	character, molded hair with ribbon and flowers, painted eyes, open mouth
1360	Alt, Beck & Gottschalck	ca 1912	"ABG", character
1361	Alt, Beck & Gottschalck	ca 1912	"ABG", character, sleep eyes, open mouth, ill. 19
1362	Alt, Beck & Gottschalck	ca 1912	"ABG", character
1366	Alt, Beck & Gottschalck	ca 1914	"ABG Made in Germany", character
1367	Alt, Beck & Gottschalck	ca 1914	character

Mold No.	Firm	Date	Description and Identification
1368	Alt, Beck & Gottschalck	ca 1914	character
	Simon & Halbig	ca 1910	"S&H", dolly face, glass eyes, open mouth, Black Doll
1370	Simon & Halbig	ca 1915	"S&H", character, also in compo or "KWG", after 1930 Keramische Werkstätten Gräfenhain formerly porcelain manufactory Simon & Halbig
1373	Alt, Beck & Gottschalck	ca 1920	character
1376	Alt, Beck Gottschalck	ca 1920	character
	Schützmeister & Quendt	ca 1920	"SQ", character
1377	unknown	ca 1915	Kewpie flange neck
1388	Simon & Halbig	ca 1910	"S&H", expressive character face, glass eyes with eye lashes of thread, open/closed smiling mouth, molded teeth
1394	Alt, Beck & Gottschalck	ca 1926	"Copr.by JL Kallus", character, flange neck, solid dome, sleep eyes, open mouth, for Geo. Borgfeldt & Co.
1397	Simon & Halbig	ca 1915	"S&H" or with "FS&Co", character, sleep eyes, open mouth, for Franz Schmidt & Co.
1398	Simon & Halbig	ca 1910	"S&H", expressive dolly face, glass eyes, eye lashes of thread, laughing mouth with tiny opening, molded teeth

Mold No.	Firm	Date	Description and Identification
1400	Robert Carl Nachf.	GM 1926	"Germany", character, flange neck, solid dome, sleep eyes, closed mouth
	Schoenau & Hoffmeister	GM 1903	"SPBH", dolly face, shoulder head
1401	Robert Carl Nachf.	GM 1926	character, baby
1402	Alt, Beck & Gottschalck	ca 1925	character
1426	Simon & Halbig	ca 1914	"S&H", character, baby
1428	Simon & Halbig	ca 1914	character, sleep eyes, open/closed mouth, ill. 1693
1429	Simon & Halbig	ca 1914	"S&H" with and without "Santa", glass eyes, open mouth, for Hamburger & Co.
1431	unknown	ca 1912	character, solid dome, glass eyes, laughing, open mouth
1432	Alt, Beck & Gottschalck	ca 1925	"Albego", character, compo
1448	Simon & Halbig	ca 1914	"S&H", character, sleep eyes, closed mouth, ill. 1694
1465	Simon & Halbig	ca 1914	"S&H", character, glass eyes, closed mouth
1468	Simon & Halbig	ca 1920	"S&H", dolly face, glass eyes, closed mouth, flapper, for Cuno & Otto Dressel
1469	Simon & Halbig	ca 1920	"S&H", dolly face, glass eyes, closed mouth, flapper, for Cuno & Otto Dressel, ill. 304

Mold No.	Firm	Date	Description and Identification
1478	Simon & Halbig	ca 1920	"S&H", character, glass eyes, closed mouth
1485	Simon & Halbig	ca 1920	"S&H", character, glass eyes, closed mouth
1488	Simon & Halbig	ca 1920	"S&H", character, glass eyes, open/closed or open mouth
1489	Simon & Halbig	ca 1925	"S&H Erika", character, sleep eyes, open mouth, presumably for Carl Hartmann, ill. 1733
1496	Simon & Halbig	ca 1920	"S&H", lady face
1498	Simon & Halbig	ca 1920	character, solid dome, painted or sleep eyes, open/closed mouth, ill. 1696
1514	Theodor Degenring	GM 1890	dolly face
1527	Simon & Halbig	ca 1925	"S&H", character, glass eyes, open/closed mouth
1563	Theodor Degenring	GM 1890	head
1565	Geo. Borgfeldt & Co.	GM 1925	"R", head
1566	Theodor Degenring	GM 1890	head
1569	Theodor Degenring	GM 1890	head
1571	Theodor Degenring	GM 1890	head
1601	Heinrich Liebermann	GM 1927	presumably "Haliso", compo
1616	Simon & Halbig	ca 1928	"S&H", character, baby, also in compo

Mold No.	Firm	Date	Description and Identification
1748	Simon & Halbig	ca 1928	"S&H", character, baby, compo
1776	Cuno & Otto Dressel	ca 1925	"CD dep", dolly face, shoulder head, glass eyes, open mouth, ill. 340 + 341
1800	Schoenau & Hoffmeister	ca 1903	"SPBH", dolly face
1813	unknown	ca 1905	dolly face, shoulder head, glass eyes, closed mouth
1848	Simon & Halbig	ca 1920	dolly face, "Jutta", for Cuno & Otto Dressel
1849	Simon & Halbig	ca 1920	dolly face, "Jutta", for Cuno & Otto Dressel
1890	Armand Marseille	ca 1890	"AM", dolly face, shoulder head
1892	Armand Marseille	ca 1892	"AM", dolly face, shoulder head
1893	Armand Marseille	GM 1892	"AM COD 93 dep", dolly face, shoulder head, for Cuno & Otto Dressel
1894	Armand Marseille	ca 1894	"AM", dolly face, shoulder or socket head
1895	Armand Marseille	ca 1895	"AM", dolly face, shoulder head
	Moritz Resek	ca 1895	"MR 175", dolly face, ill.2032
1896	Armand Marseille	ca 1896	"AM", dolly face, shoulder head, also made for Cuno & Otto Dressel
1897	Armand Marseille	ca 1897	"AM", dolly face, shoulder or socket head

Mold No.	Firm	Date	Description and Identification
1898	Armand Marseille	ca 1898	"AM", dolly face, shoulder head, also made for Cuno & Otto Dressel
1899	Armand Marseille	ca 1899	"AM", dolly face, shoulder head
	Peter Scherf	ca 1899	"PSch", dolly face, shoulder head
	Wenzel Prouza	ca 1899	"WEP", dolly face
1900	Armand Marseille	ca 1900	"AM", dolly face
	Ernst Heubach	ca 1900	with horseshoe, dolly face, shoulder head, ill. color 58 + ill. 684
	Schoenau & Hoffmeister	ca 1900	"AS", dolly face, glass eyes, open mouth, for Arthur Schoenau, ill. 1618
	unknown	ca 1900	"No", shoulder head, molded hair, painted eyes, closed mouth
1901	Armand Marseille	ca 1901	"AM", dolly face, shoulder head
	Peter Scherf	ca 1901	"PSch", dolly face, shoulder head
	Ernst Heubach	ca 1901	with horseshoe, dolly face, shoulder head
1902	Armand Marseille	ca 1902	"AM", dolly face, shoulder head
	Peter Scherf	ca 1902	"PSch", dolly face, shoulder head
	Ernst Heubach	ca 1902	with horseshoe, dolly face, shoulder head
	unknown	ca 1902	dolly face, glass eyes, open mouth

Mold No.	Firm	Date	Description and Identification
1903	Armand Marseille	ca 1903	"AM", dolly face, shoulder head
	Adolf Prouza	ca 1910	"AP", dolly face, **ill. 2031**
	Pollack & Hoffmann	ca 1903	"P&H", dolly face
1904	Schoenau & Hoffmeister	ca 1904	"SPBH", dolly face
	Erste Steinbacher Porzellanfabrik Gustav Heubach	ca 1925	"GH", dolly face, shoulder or socket head
	Pollack & Hoffmann	ca 1904	"P&H", dolly face, **ill. 2030**
	A.C. Anger	ca 1920	"AeM", dolly face, **ill. 2025** or "Eduardo Juan", dolly face, **ill. 2026**
1905	Armand Marseille	ca 1905	"AM", dolly face, shoulder head
1906	Ernst Heubach	ca 1906	with horseshoe, dolly face, shoulder head
	Schoenau & Hoffmeister	ca 1906	"SPBH", dolly face
1907	Theodor Recknagel	GM 1910	"DEP RA", dolly face
	Theodor Pohl	ca 1907	"TP", dolly face
	Plass & Roesner	ca 1907	"P&R", dolly face, **ill. 2028**
1909	Schoenau & Hoffmeister	ca 1909	"SPBH" in star, dolly face
	Armand Marseille	ca 1909	"AM", dolly face, shoulder head
	Ernst Heubach	ca 1909	with horseshoe, dolly face, shoulder head
	Theodor Recknagel	ca 1910	"DEP RA", dolly face, glass eyes, open mouth, **ill. 1450**
1910	Ernst Winkler	ca 1910	"W", dolly face

Mold No.	Firm	Date	Description and Identification
1910	unknown	ca 1910	"Taft", dolly face, glass eyes, open mouth
1912	Simon & Halbig	ca 1912	"S&H Jutta", dolly face, for Cuno & Otto Dressel
	unknown	ca 1912	"Germany", dolly face, sleep eyes, open mouth, ill. 2073
1913	Plass & Roesner	ca 1913	"PR ROMA", dolly face, ill.2029
	Heinrich Bätz	GM 1913	head
1914	Simon & Halbig	ca 1914	"S&H Jutta", character, for Cuno & Otto Dressel, ill. 303
	Theodor Recknagel	ca 1914	"Dep RA", dolly face
	Heinrich Bätz	GM 1913	head
	unknown	ca 1914	"Germany", dolly face, sleep eyes, open mouth
1916	Simon & Halbig	ca 1925	"S&H", character, compo
	C.M. Bergmann	ca 1916	dolly face, sleep eyes, ill. 123
1920	Simon & Halbig	ca 1920	"S&H Jutta", character, for Cuno & Otto Dressel
1920	August Möller & Sohn	ca 1920	"Amuso", character
1922	Ernst Heubach	ca 1922	"Jutta-Baby Dressel", character, sleep eyes, open mouth, for Cuno & Otto Dressel
1923	presumable Ma.E. Maar	ca 1923	"M", character, sleep eyes, open mouth
1924	Theodor Recknagel	ca 1924	"RA", character
	Hermann Pensky	ca 1924	"Hannelore PH", character, sleep eyes, open mouth

Mold No.	Firm	Date	Description and Identification
1930	Schoenau & Hoffmeister	ca 1930	"Porzellanfabrik Burggrub Das lachende Baby", character, sleep eyes, open laughing mouth, ill. 1625
2000	Nikolaus Oberender	ca 1911	"NO", character, shoulder head, solid dome, painted eyes, closed mouth
	Armand Marseille	GM 1895	head
2010	Nikolaus Oberender	ca 1911	"NO", character, shoulder head, solid dome, painted eyes, closed mouth
	Armand Marseille	GM 1896	"AM", dolly face
2015	Armand Marseille	GM 1896	"W" with anchor, dolly face, shoulder head, glass eyes, closed mouth, presumably for Louis Wolf & Co., ill. color 90
2020	Baehr & Proeschild	ca 1912	"BSW" incised heart, "482", character, solid dome, sleep eyes, open mouth, for Bruno Schmidt
2023	Baehr & Proeschild	ca 1912	"BSW" incised heart, "539", character, solid dome, painted eyes, closed mouth, for Bruno Schmidt
2025	Baehr & Proeschild	ca 1912	"BSW" incised heart, "539", character, solid dome or with wig, painted eyes, closed mouth, for Bruno Schmidt, ill. 1557
2033	Baehr & Proeschild	ca 1912	"BSW" incised heart, "537", character, sleep eyes, closed mouth, for Bruno Schmidt
2042	Baehr & Proeschild	ca 1912	"BSW" incised heart, character, solid dome, painted eyes, open/closed mouth

Mold No.	Firm	Date	Description and Identification
2048	Baehr & Proeschild	ca 1212	with and without "BSW" incised heart, character, solid dome, sleep eyes, open or closed mouth
2070	Baehr & Proeschild	ca 1920	character
2072	Baehr & Proeschild	ca 1920	"BSW" incised heart, character, sleep eyes, open or closed mouth, for Bruno Schmidt
2074	Baehr & Proeschild	GM 1927	character, for Bruno Schmidt
2075	Baehr & Proeschild	GM 1927	character, for Bruno Schmidt
2081	Baehr & Proeschild	ca 1920	character
2084	Baehr & Proeschild	ca 1920	"BP" with crossed swords, character, solid dome, sleep eyes, open mouth, for Bruno Schmidt
2085	Baehr & Proeschild	ca 1920	"BSW" incised heart, character, sleep eyes, open mouth, for Bruno Schmidt or "BP" with crossed swords, otherwise as before
2092	Baehr & Proeschild	ca 1920	character, baby, for Bruno Schmidt
2094	Baehr & Proeschild	ca 1920	"BSW" incised heart, character, solid dome, sleep eyes, open mouth, for Bruno Schmidt, ill. 1544
2095	Baehr & Proeschild	ca 1920	"BSW" incised heart, character, solid dome, sleep eyes, open mouth, for Bruno Schmidt
2096	Baehr & Proeschild	ca 1920	"BSW" incised heart, character, solid dome, sleep eyes, open mouth, for Bruno Schmidt

Mold No.	Firm	Date	Description and Identification
2097	Baehr & Proeschild	GM 1911	"BSW" incised heart, character as bent—limb baby or toddler, for Buno Schmidt or "BP" with crossed swords, otherwise as before
2099	Baehr & Proeschild	ca 1920	"BS" incised heart, "678", character, baby, for Bruno Schmidt
2144	Paul Rauschert	GM 1930	"D", character
2154	Baehr & Proeschild	ca 1920	jointed doll
2500	Schoenau & Hoffmeister	ca 1905	"SPBH", dolly face
2542	Armand Marseille	ca 1930	"AM", character, solid dome, sleep eyes, open mouth or "SP" in circle, successor of Armand Marseille after 1948 Sonneberger Porzellanfabriken , compo
2918	Geo. Borgfeldt & Co.	GM 1924	newborn
2966	Sonneberger Porzellanfabriken	ca 1948	"SP" in circle, sleep eyes, open mouth, compo
3066	Armand Marseille	ca 1895	"AM", dolly face, shoulder head
3091	Armand Marseille	ca 1896	"AM", dolly face, shoulder head
3093	Armand Marseille	ca 1896	"AM", dolly face, shoulder head
3095	Armand Marseille	ca 1896	"AM", dolly face, shoulder head

Mold No.	Firm	Date	Description and Identification
3200	Armand Marseille	GM 1896	"AM", dolly face, shoulder head, ill. color 91 + ill.1743 + 1744
3300	Armand Marseille	ca 1896	"AM", dolly face, shoulder head
3500	Armand Marseille	GM 1899	"AM", dolly face, shoulder head
3600	Armand Marseille	ca 1899	"AM DEP", dolly face
3700	Armand Marseille	ca 1899	"AM", dolly face, shoulder head
4000	Schoenau & Hoffmeister	ca 1905	"SPBH", dolly face
4001	Schoenau & Hoffmeister	ca 1905	"SPBH", dolly face
4008	Armand Marseille	ca 1900	"AM", dolly face, shoulder head
4129	Nöckler & Tittel	GM 1923	"P" or "H", jointed doll, trademark "Schneeflöckchen"
4500	Schoenau & Hoffmeister	ca 1905	"SPBH", dolly face
4536	Paul Schmidt	ca 1923	"PS", character
4600	Schoenau & Hoffmeister	ca 1905	"SPBH", dolly face
4700	Schoenau & Hoffmeister	ca 1905	"SPBH", dolly face, shoulder head
4703	Weiss, Kühnert & Co.	ca 1913	character
4900	Schoenau & Hoffmeister	ca 1905	"SPBH", dolly face, Oriental, ill. 1619

Mold No.	Firm	Date	Description and Identification
5000	Schoenau & Hoffmeister	GM 1903	"SPBH", dolly face
5300	Schoenau & Hoffmeister	ca 1905	"SPBH", dolly face
5430	Porzellanfabrik Rauenstein	GM 1910	sulky child
5431	Porzellanfabrik Rauenstein	GM 1910	laughing face
5500	Schoenau & Hoffmeister	ca 1905	"SPBH", dolly face
5625	Gebr. Heubach	ca 1912	with sun, character, glass eyes, laughing
5636	Gebr. Heubach	ca 1912	with sun, character, glass eyes, laughing, open/closed mouth with two molded teeth
5689	Gebr. Heubach	ca 1912	with sun, character, glass eyes, open mouth
5700	Schoenau & Hoffmeister	ca 1905	"SPBH", dolly face
5730	Gebr. Heubach	ca 1912	with sun, character, sleep eyes, open mouth, "Santa", for Hamburger & Co
5773	Gebr. Heubach	ca 1912	character, shoulder head
5777	Gebr. Heubach	ca 1913	with sun and "Dolly Dimple", character, sleep eyes, open mouth, for Hamburger & Co., ill. 531
5800	Schoenau & Hoffmeister	ca 1905	"SPBH", dolly face
6399	Geo. Borgfeldt & Co.	GM 1926	head with bobbed hair

Mold No.	Firm	Date	Description and Identificatio
6600	Paul Rauschert	GM 1910	"PR" with "I" or "II", character
6688	Gebr. Heubach	ca 1912	character, shoulder head, solid dome, painted eyes, closed mouth
6692	Gebr. Heubach	ca 1912	with sun, character, shoulder head, painted eyes, closed mouth, boy
6736	Gebr. Heubach	ca 1912	with square, character, shoulder head, painted eyes, laughing, boy
6774	Gebr. Heubach	ca 1913	with square, character, painted eyes, whistling,"Whistling Jim"
6789	Walther & Sohn	ca 1922	"W&S", character
	Otto Gans	ca 1922	"OG", character
6891	Gebr. Heubach	ca 1912	character, painted eyes, closed mouth
6892	Gebr. Heubach	ca 1912	with sun, character, shoulder head, painted eyes, closed mouth, boy
6894	Gebr. Heubach	ca 1912	character, painted eyes, closed mouth, boy
6896	Gebr. Heubach	ca 1912	character, painted eyes, closed mouth
6897	Gebr. Heubach	ca 1912	character, painted eyes, laughing, boy
6969	Gebr. Heubach	ca 1912	with square, character, glass eyes, closed mouth, ill. color 61

Mold No.	Firm	Date	Description and Identification
6970	Gebr. Heubach	ca 1912	with sun, character, glass eyes, closed mouth
6971	Gebr. Heubach	ca 1912	with sun, character, painted eyes, laughing
7027	Gebr. Heubach	ca 1912	with sun, character, boy
7064	Gebr. Heubach	ca 1912	character, painted eyes, smiling
7072	Gebr. Heubach	ca 1912	with sun, character, painted eyes, closed mouth, boy
7077	Gebr. Heubach	ca 1912	with sun, character with molded bonnet, painted eyes, closed mouth, girl
7106	Gebr. Heubach	ca 1912	with sun, character, painted eyes, laughing, boy
7109	Gebr. Heubach	ca 1912	with sun, character, painted eyes, open/closed mouth, ill.723
7124	Gebr. Heubach	ca 1912	with sun, character, shoulder head, painted eyes, open/closed mouth
7129	Gebr. Heubach	GM 1910	with sun, character, painted eyes, laughing, boy
7134	Gebr. Heubach	GM 1910	character, shoulder head, painted eyes, crying, boy
7138	Gebr. Heubach	ca 1910	character, sleep eyes, closed mouth
7139	Gebr. Heubach	GM 1910	with square, character, shoulder head, painted eyes, open/closed mouth, girl

Mold No.	Firm	Date	Description and Identification
7144	Gebr. Heubach	ca 1910	character, painted eyes, closed mouth, ill. 708
7211	Gebr. Heubach	ca 1910	with square, character, painted eyes, open/closed laughing mouth
7226	Gebr. Heubach	ca 1910	with square, character, molded bonnet, painted eyes, closed mouth, girl
7246	Gebr. Heubach	ca 1912	with sun or square, character, sleep eyes, closed mouth
7247	Gebr. Heubach	ca 1912	with sun, character, glass eyes, closed mouth
7248	Gebr. Heubach	ca 1912	character, glass eyes, closed mouth
7256	Gebr. Heubach	ca 1912	character, glass eyes, closed mouth
7307	Gebr. Heubach	ca 1912	character, painted eyes, laughing
7314	Gebr. Heubach	ca 1912	with square, character, painted eyes, laughing
7326	Gebr. Heubach	ca 1912	shoulder head, lady doll
7345	Gebr. Heubach	ca 1912	with sun, character, shoulder head, painted eyes, smiling, boy
7346	Gebr. Heubach	ca 1912	with sun or square, character, shoulder head, glass eyes, closed mouth

Mold No.	Firm	Date	Description and Identification
7402	Gebr. Heubach	ca 1912	character, painted eyes, laughing
7407	Gebr. Heubach	ca 1912	character, glass eyes, open/closed mouth
7550	Gebr. Heubach	ca 1912	character, sleep eyes, open/closed mouth with molded tongue
7587	Gebr. Heubach	ca 1914	with square, character, painted googly eyes, closed mouth
7602	Gebr. Heubach	ca 1912	with sun or square, character, painted eyes, closed mouth, (ca 1930 also made in compo), **ill. color 4**
7603	Gebr. Heubach	ca 1912	with sun, character, painted eyes, closed mouth
7604	Gebr. Heubach	ca 1912	with sun or square, character, painted eyes, laughing, open/closed mouth or with glass eyes, wig, boy, **ill. color 65**
7614	Gebr. Heubach	ca 1912	with square, character, painted eyes, boy
7616	Gebr. Heubach	ca 1912	character, shoulder head, glass eyes, open/closed mouth
7620	Gebr. Heubach	ca 1912	with square or sun, character, painted eyes, open/closed mouth, also made as Black Doll
7622	Gebr. Heubach	ca 1912	with sun, character, painted eyes, closed mouth, boy

Mold No.	Firm	Date	Description and Identification
7623	Gebr. Heubach	ca 1912	with sun, character, painted eyes, open/closed mouth
7624	Gebr. Heubach	GM 1910	character
7625	Gebr. Heubach	GM 1910	character
7631	Gebr. Heubach	ca 1912	character, painted eyes, closed mouth, boy
7634	Gebr. Heubach	ca 1912	with sun, character, painted eyes, crying, boy
7635	Gebr. Heubach	GM 1910	character
7636	Gebr. Heubach	GM 1910	character
7637	Gebr. Heubach	ca 1912	with sun, character, painted eyes, smiling
7644	Gebr. Heubach	GM 1910	with sun or square, character, shoulder head, painted eyes, laughing, boy
7647	Gebr. Heubach	ca 1912	with sun, character, painted eyes, open/closed laughing mouth
7650	Gebr. Heubach	ca 1912	character, glass eyes, open/closed mouth
7657	Gebr. Heubach	GM 1910	character
7658	Gebr. Heubach	GM 1910	character
7659	Gebr. Heubach	GM 1910	character

Mold No.	Firm	Date	Description and Identification
7669	Gebr. Heubach	ca 1912	with sun, character, glass eyes, open/closed mouth, often found on mechanical walking dolls, **ill. 701**
7670	Gebr. Heubach	ca 1912	with sun, character, Black Doll
7671	Gebr. Heubach	ca 1912	with sun, character, Black Doll
7679	Gebr. Heubach	ca 1912	character, glass eyes, open/closed mouth
7686	Gebr. Heubach	GM 1911	character, glass eyes, open/closed mouth with molded tongue
7687	Gebr. Heubach	GM 1911	character
7692	Gebr. Heubach	GM 1911	character
7701	Gebr. Heubach	GM 1911	character
7703	Gebr. Heubach	ca 1911	with sun, character, molded hair with bow, painted eyes, laughing, **ill. 705**
7711	Gebr. Heubach	ca 1912	with sun, character, glass eyes, open mouth
7714	Gebr. Heubach	GM 1911	character
7739	Gebr. Heubach	GM 1911	character
7740	Gebr. Heubach	GM 1911	character
7743	Gebr. Heubach	ca 1912	with sun, character, painted eyes, smiling, open/closed mouth, boy

Mold No.	Firm	Date	Description and Identification
7744	Gebr. Heubach	ca 1912	with sun, character, painted eyes, closed pouty mouth, boy
7745	Gebr. Heubach	ca 1912	with sun, character, painted eyes, laughing, boy,ill. 709
7759	Gebr. Heubach	ca 1912	with sun or square, character, painted eyes, closed mouth
7760	Gebr. Heubach	ca 1912	with sun, character, painted eyes, closed mouth, boy
7761	Gebr. Heubach	ca 1912	with sun, character, painted eyes, open/closed mouth, grumbling, crying (see shoulder head mold # 7843)
7763	Gebr. Heubach	ca 1912	with sun or square, character, molded hair with bow, painted eyes, closed mouth, girl
7764	Gebr. Heubach	ca 1912	with square, character, molded hair with bow, painted eyes, large open/closed mouth, singing girl
7768	Gebr. Heubach	ca 1912	with square, molded hair with bow, character, painted eyes, closed mouth, girl
7779	Gebr. Heubach	ca 1912	with sun, character, molded bonnet, painted eyes, closed mouth
7788	Gebr. Heubach	ca 1912	with square, character, molded hair with bow
7843	Gebr. Heubach	ca 1912	with square, shoulder head, (see mold # 7761)

138

Mold No.	Firm	Date	Description and Identification
7850	Gebr. Heubach	ca 1912	with square, character, shoulder head, molded hair with bow, painted eyes, closed mouth, girl
7851	Gebr. Heubach	ca 1912	with square, character, (see mold # 7850)
7864	Gebr. Heubach	ca 1912	character, shoulder head, glass eyes, closed mouth
7867	Gebr. Heubach	ca 1912	with square, character, shoulder head, molded braids, painted eyes, closed mouth, girl or with socket head, otherwise as before, ill. 702
7885	Gebr. Heubach	ca 1912	with square, character, molded hair, bow, painted eyes, closed mouth, ill. color 62
7890	Gebr. Heubach	ca 1912	character, molded hair, bow, painted eyes, girl
7911	Gebr. Heubach	ca 1912	character, painted eyes, laughing, open/closed mouth, boy
7925	Gebr. Heubach	ca 1914	character, shoulder head, glass eyes, smiling, open mouth, lady doll, ill. 703
7926	Gebr. Heubach	ca 1912	character, shoulder head, glass eyes, smiling, open mouth, lady doll
7956	Gebr. Heubach	ca 1912	with square, character, molded hair, painted eyes, closed mouth, girl
7971	Gebr. Heubach	ca 1912	character, painted eyes, laughing, boy

Mold No.	Firm	Date	Description and Identification
7975	Gebr. Heubach	ca 1912	with sun or square, molded take off bonnet made of bisque with painted roses or rose coloured bonnet with painted yellow ribbon, sleep eyes, closed mouth
7977	Gebr. Heubach	ca 1912	with sun or square, character, molded bonnet, painted eyes, closed mouth, ill. 700
7917	Gebr. Heubach	ca 1914	with sun, character, sleep eyes, closed mouth
8017	Gebr. Heubach	ca 1912	"Germany", character, glass eyes, closed mouth
8050	Gebr. Heubach	ca 1912	character, painted eyes, laughing, girl
8055	Gebr. Heubach	ca 1912	with square, character, shoulder head, painted eyes, laughing, closed mouth
8173	Kämmer & Reinhardt	GM 1925	"K&R/S&H", flange neck, newborn, "Klein-Mammy", (see mold # 173)
8191	Gebr. Heubach	ca 1912	with square, character, painted eyes, laughing, boy
8192	Gebr. Heubach	ca 1914	with sun or square, character, sleep eyes, open mouth
8195	Gebr. Heubach	ca 1912	with square, character, shoulder head, painted eyes, closed mouth, boy
8226	Gebr. Heubach	ca 1912	with square, character, shoulder head, molded bonnet, painted eyes, closed mouth, girl

Mold No.	Firm	Date	Description and Identification
8232	Gebr. Heubach	ca 1914	character, shoulder head, glass eyes, open mouth
8306	Gebr. Heubach	ca 1912	with square, character, shoulder head, painted eyes, laughing, boy
8309	Gebr. Heubach	ca 1912	with square, character, painted eyes, laughing, boy
8407	Gebr. Heubach	ca 1912	with square, character, glass eyes, closed mouth
8413	Gebr. Heubach	ca 1914	with square, character, sleep eyes, open/closed mouth
8316	Gebr. Heubach	ca 1914	with square, character, glass eyes, laughing
8420	Gebr. Heubach	ca 1914	with square, character, sleep eyes, open mouth
8457	Gebr. Heubach	ca 1913	with square, character, shoulder head, Red Indian
8459	Gebr. Heubach	ca 1914	character, sleep eyes, laughing
8473	Gebr. Heubach	ca 1914	with square, character, glass eyes, open/closed mouth
8547	Gebr. Heubach	ca 1912	with square, character, shoulder head, painted eyes, closed mouth, girl
8548	Gebr. Heubach	ca 1912	with square, character, painted or glass eyes, closed pouty mouth, ill. 710

Mold No.	Firm	Date	Description and Identification
8552	Limbach AG.	ca 1911	with clover-leaf, shoulder head, lady doll, with molded ribbon, painted eyes, open/closed mouth with molded teeth, molded blouse
8553	Limbach AG.	ca 1911	with clover-leaf, shoulder head, lady doll, with molded ribbon
8572	Gebr. Heubach	ca 1912	character, painted eyes, open/closed mouth
8588	Gebr. Heubach	ca 1912	with square, character, painted eyes, closed pouty mouth
8589	Gebr. Heubach	ca 1914	with square, character, painted googly eyes, closed mouth
8606	Gebr. Heubach	ca 1914	character, painted googly eyes, closed mouth
8682	Limbach AG.	ca 1911	with clover-leaf, character, molded hair, painted or glass eyes, open/closed mouth, ill. 1119
8724	Gebr. Heubach	ca 1914	character, shoulder head, painted eyes, closed mouth
8729	Gebr. Heubach	ca 1914	with square, character, painted googly eyes, closed mouth
8759	Gebr. Heubach	ca 1914	with square, character, molded baby cap, painted eyes, open/closed mouth with molded tongue
8764	Gebr. Heubach	ca 1914	"EINCO", character, shoulder head, googly eyes, closed mouth, for Eisenmann & Co.

Mold No.	Firm	Date	Description and Identification
8774	Gebr. Heubach	ca 1914	with sun or square, character, painted eyes, whistling, "Whistling Jim"
8778	Gebr. Heubach	GM 1913	grandmother
8801	Gebr. Heubach	ca 1914	character, shoulder head, painted eyes, laughing, ill. 706
8867	Limbach AG.	ca 1926	newborn, for Louis Amberg & Son
8878	Gebr. Heubach	ca 1914	with square, character, painted eyes, laughing, boy
9042	Gebr. Heubach	ca 1914	character, shoulder head
9056	Gebr. Heubach	ca 1914	with square, character, painted googly eyes, closed mouth
9072	Gebr. Heubach	ca 1914	character, painted eyes, closed mouth, boy
9081	Gebr. Heubach	ca 1914	character, painted googly eyes, closed mouth
9085	Gebr. Heubach	ca 1914	with square, character, solid dome with hole for a real curl or plait, painted googly eyes, closed mouth
9141	Gebr. Heubach	ca 1914	with square, character, right painted googly eye, left eye winking, closed mouth, ill. 712
9167	Gebr. Heubach	ca 1914	with square, character, painted eyes, closed mouth

Mold No.	Firm	Date	Description and Identification
9209	Gebr. Heubach	ca 1914	with square, clown's head, ill. 721
9219	Gebr. Heubach	ca 1914	character, painted eyes, closed mouth
9355	Gebr. Heubach	ca 1914	with square, character, shoulder head, sleep eyes, open mouth
9457	Gebr. Heubach	ca 1914	with square, character, expressive face, old man with Eskimo or Red Indian features, ill. 390 + 706
9500	Rudolph Heinz & Co.	ca 1922	"AV Neuhaus am Rwg.", dolly face, ill. 602
9513	Gebr. Heubach	ca 1914	with square, character, googly eyes, closed mouth
9572	Gebr. Heubach	ca 1914	with square, character, googly eyes, closed mouth
9578	Gebr. Heubach	ca 1914	with square, character, googly eyes, closed mouth
9594	Gebr. Heubach	ca 1914	with square, character, painted googly eyes, closed mouth
10532	Gebr. Heubach	ca 1920	with square, character, sleep eyes, open mouth
10539	Gebr. Heubach	ca 1920	with square, character, baby, sleep eyes, open mouth, for Wagner & Zetsche
10556	Gebr. Heubach	ca 1920	with square, character, (see mold # 10539)

Mold No.	Firm	Date	Description and Identification
10557	Gebr. Heubach	ca 1920	with square, character, (see mold # 10539)
10586	Gebr. Heubach	ca 1920	with square, character, (see mold # 10539)
10588	Gebr. Heubach	ca 1920	with square, character, (see mold # 10539)
10617	Gebr. Heubach	ca 1920	character, sleep eyes, open mouth
10633	Gebr. Heubach	ca 1922	with square, character, shoulder head, glass eyes, open mouth, Dainty Dorothy
10727	Gebr. Heubach	ca 1922	with square, character, sleep eyes, open mouth, "REVALO", for Gebr.Ohlhaver
10731	Gebr. Heubach	ca 1920	"Mirette", character, sleep eyes, open mouth
10790	Gebr. Heubach	ca 1920	with square, character
11010	Gebr. Heubach	ca 1922	character, sleep eyes, open mouth, "REVALO", for Gebr. Ohlhaver
12386	Gebr. Heubach	ca 1925	with square, character, baby
13765	Geo. Borgfeldt & Co.	GM 1923	character head
19251	Ernst Winkler	GM 1926	head
19252	Ernst Winkler	GM 1926	head

DRP and DRGM Numbers of Trademarks or Stamps that can be found on bodies

Registration No.	DRP or DRGM	Year	Firm
5 332	DRGM	1892	Johannes Franz, Sonneberg
16 647	DRGM	1893	Hermann Wegner, Sonneberg
19 555	DRGM	1893	Franz Schmidt, Georgenthal
43 594	DRGM	1895	Richard Fröber, Hüttensteinach
46 547	DRP	1888	Josef Bergmann, Sonneberg
56 562	DRP	1890	Simon & Halbig, Gräfenhain
56 996	DRP	1890	Gottlieb Zinner, Schalkau
66 534	DRP	1892	Hermann Landshut & Co., Waltershausen
70 685	DRP	1893	J.D. Kestner jr., Waltershausen
78 281	DRP	1894	Reinhold Weingart jr.(see Alt, Beck & Gottschalck and Franz Schmidt)
100 279	DRP	1897	Heinrich Handwerck, Waltershausen
119 857	DRP	1900	Ferdinand Imhoff, Berlin
132 410	DRGM	1900	Robert Carl, Köppelsdorf
EP 134 769	GM	1913	Armand Marseille, Köppelsdorf
160 638	DRGM	1901	Alfred Heller, Meiningen
193 440	DRGM	1903	Louis Stammberger, Schalkau
201 013	DRGM	1903	Louis Liebermann, Sonneberg
357 529	DRGM	1908	Hermann Wegner, Sonneberg
374 830	DRGM	1909	Armand Marseille, Köppelsdorf
374 831	DRGM	1909	Armand Marseille, Köppelsdorf
377 439	DRGM	1909	Armand Marseille, Köppelsdorf
421 481	DRGM	1911	Adolf Wislizenus, Waltershausen
441 857	DRGM	1910	F.M. Schilling, Sonneberg
442 910	DRGM	1910	Rudolf Walch, Unterweid
447 828	DRGM	1910	Rheinische Gummi- und Celluloid Fabrik, Mannheim-Neckarau

Registration No.	DRP or DRGM	Year	Firm
452 711	DRGM	1911	Wiesenthal, Schindel & Kallenberg, Waltershausen
486 986	DRGM	1911	Franz Belouscheck (Heubach, Lichte)
520 942	DRGM	1912	Alt, Beck & Gottschalck, Nauendorf
657 708	DRGM	1916	Wagner & Zetsche, Ilmenau
856 346	DRGM	1923	Johann Müller, Nürnberg
897 388	DRGM	1924	Louis Reber, Sonneberg
945 354	DRGM	1925	Priska Sander, Neustadt/Orla
954 642	DRGM	1926	Hermann Steiner, Neustadt/Coburg
1 125 389	DRGM	1930	Gebr. Süssenguth, Neustadt/Coburg

The following Letters were found as abbreviations
on doll heads, also a few on doll bodies. These
markings are either marks, trademarks or labels of doll
factories, porcelain manufactories or import houses.

Letter	Firm
A	
ABG	Alt, Beck & Gottschalck, Nauendorf
AF&C	Fleischmann & Craemer, Sonneberg
AH	Adolf Heller, Waltershausen
AHS	Albin Steiner, Schalkau
AHW	Adolf Heller, Waltershausen
AHW	Adolf Hülss, Waltershausen
AK	A. Kröhl, Berlin
ALB	Adolf Landsberger, Magdeburg
ALS	Anton Link, Saulgau
AM	Armand Marseille, Köppelsdorf
AM	A. Michaelis, Rauenstein
AeM	A.C. Anger, Bohemia
AMN	Andreas Müller, Sonneberg
AP	Adolf Prouza, Bohemia
AR	Theodor Recknagel, Alexandrinenthal
AR	August Riedeler, Königsee
AS	Arthur Schoenau, Sonneberg
AS	August Steiner, Köppelsdorf
ASS	Arthur Schoenau, Sonneberg
AV	Porzellanfabrik Neuhaus am Rennsteig

Letter	Firm
B	
BJ&Co	B. Illfelder & Co., Fürth/New York City
BP	Baehr & Proeschild, Ohrdruf
BP	Swaine & Co., Hüttensteinach
B&P	Baehr & Proeschild, Ohrdruf
BS	Bruno Schmidt, Waltershausen
BSW	Bruno Schmidt, Waltershausen
C	
C	Cuno & Otto Dressel, Sonneberg
C	Dressel & Koch, Köppelsdorf
CB	Carl Bergmann, Sonneberg
CC	unknown
CEGD	C. Erich Günther, Dresden
CE&S	Christian Eichhorn & Söhne, Steinach
CEUS	Christian Eichhorn & Söhne, Steinach
CF&Co	Carl Feiler & Co., Jena
CH	Carl Hartmann, Neustadt
CHND	Carl Horn Nachf., Dresden
CK	Carl Knoll, Bohemia
CKF	Carl Krahmer, Frankenhausen
COD	Cuno & Otto Dressel, Sonneberg
CP	Catterfelder Puppenfabrik, Catterfeld
C&S	Curnen & Steiner, Sonneberg
CT	Carl Trautmann, Finsterbergen
CV	Closter Veilsdorf
D	
D	Julius Dorst, Sonneberg

Letter	Firm
D I	Swaine & Co., Hüttensteinach
DEP	= deponiert, -) DEP
DGMSch	= Deutscher Gebrauchs-Muster-Schutz, -) DGMSch
DIP	Swaine & Co., Hüttensteinach
D&K	Dressel & Koch, Köppelsdorf
DKF	Dornheim, Koch & Fischer, Gräfenroda
D&PC	Dressel & Pietschmann, Coburg
D.P.	Hamburger & Co., Berlin/New York City
DP	Dora Petzold, Berlin
DRGM	= Deutsches Reichs-Gebrauchs-Muster, -) DRGM
DRMR	= Deutsche Reichs-Muster-Rolle, -) DRMR
DRP	= Deutsches Reichs-Patent, -) DRP
DV	Swaine & Co., Hüttensteinach

E

EBVR	Emil Bauersachs, Sonneberg
ED	E. Dehler, Coburg
ED	Cuno & Otto Dressel, Sonneberg
D	Cuno & Otto Dressel, Sonneberg
EDH	E. Dehler, Coburg
EG	Edgard Goldstein & Co., Berlin
EG	Ernst Großmann, Sonneberg
EH	Ernst Heubach, Köppelsdorf
EHK	Ernst Heubach, Köppelsdorf
EK	Ernst Klötzer, Sonneberg
EK	Edmund Knoch, Mönchröden
EL	Ernst Liebermann, Neustadt
EM	Ernst Metzler, Pressig-Rothenkirchen
EP	Emil Pfeiffer, Vienna
E&S	Christian Eichhorn & Söhne, Steinach
ESTP	Erste Steinbacher Porzellanfabrik, Steinbach

Letter	Firm
EUST	Edmund Ulrich Steiner, Sonneberg
EvB	Erich von Berg, Steinach
EW	Ernst Winkler, Sonneberg
EWH	Ernst Wehncke, Hamburg
EZ	Emil Zitzmann, Steinach

F

FB	Fritz Bierschenk, Sonneberg
F&B	Fleischmann & Bloedel, Fürth
F&BF	Fleischmann & Bloedel, Fürth
FEWB	Fried. Edm. Winkler, Sonneberg
FNC	Fischer, Naumann & Co., Ilmenau
FNI	Fischer, Naumann & Co., Ilmenau
FN&Co	Fischer, Naumann & Co., Ilmenau
FP	Friedrichsrodaer Puppenfabrik
FP	Swaine & Co., Hüttensteinach
FS	Franz Schmidt & Co., Georgenthal
FS&Co	Franz Schmidt & Co., Georgenthal
FWB	F. Welsch, Breslau

G

G	Georg Gebert, Berlin
GB	Geo. Borgfeldt & Co., Berlin
GbrK	Gebr. Kühnlenz, Kronach
G&Co	Greiner & Co., Steinach
GDF	unknown
GH	Gustav Heubach, Steinbach
GH	Gebr. Heubach, Lichte
GK	Gebr. Kühnlenz, Kronach
GKN	Gebr. Knoch, Neustadt

Letter	Firm
GL	Georg Lutz, Sonneberg
GL	unknown
GM	= Geschmacks-Muster-Schutz, -) GM
GMS	= Gebrauchs-Muster-Schutz, -) DRGM
GS	Gans & Seyfarth, Waltershausen
GS	Gebr. Süssenguth, Neustadt
G&S	Gutmann & Schiffnie, Nürnberg
G&S	Gans & Seyfarth, Waltershausen
GT	Gerber & Teusch, Sonneberg
GW	Gustav Wohlleben, Neustadt

H

Letter	Firm
H	Heinrich Handwerck, Waltershausen
HC	Heber & Co., Neustadt
HcHH	Heinrich Handwerck, Waltershausen
H&Co	Hamburger & Co., Nürnberg/New York City
HH	Hermann Heyde, Dresden
HH	Heinrich Handwerck, Waltershausen
HHD	Hermann Heyde, Dresden
HHW	Heinrich Handwerck, Waltershausen
HJL	H.J. Leven, Sonneberg
HL	unknown
HPF	Herzpuppen-Fabrik, Berlin
HS	Hermann Steiner, Neustadt
HSN	Hermann Steiner, Neustadt
HSt	Hermann Steiner, Neustadt
HW	Heinrich Handwerck, Waltershausen
HWENSPF	Hermann Wolf, Nordhausen
HWN	Hugo Wiegand, Waltershausen

Letter	Firm
I	
IB	Iris Beaumont, Berlin
J	
JDK	J.D. Kestner jr., Waltershausen
JDS	Julius Dorst, Sonneberg
JH&S	Julius Hering & Sohn, Köppelsdorf
JIO	Alt, Beck & Gottschalck, Nauendorf
JK	Theodor Recknagel, Alexandrinenthal
JMS	Julia Müller-Sarne, Dresden
K	
KB	unknown
K&Co	Kestner & Comp., Ohrdruf
KH	Karl Hartmann, Stockheim
K&H	Kley & Hahn, Ohrdruf
KK	Käthe Kruse, Bad Kösen
KPM	Königl. Porzellanmanufaktur Meissen
KPM	Königl. Porzellanmanufaktur Berlin
KPM	A.W.Fr. Kistner, Scheibe
KPN	Karl Pietsch, Oeslau
KR	Kämmer & Reinhardt, Waltershausen
K&R	Kämmer & Reinhardt, Waltershausen
KW	Kohl & Wengenroth, Offenbach
K&W	Koch & Weithase, Köppelsdorf
K&W	Koenig & Wernicke, Waltershausen
KWW	Koenig & Wernicke, Waltershausen

Letter	Firm

L

LA&S	Louis Amberg & Son, Sonneberg/New York City
LD	Löffler & Dill, Sonneberg
L&D	Löffler & Dill, Sonneberg
L&DS	Löffler & Dill, Sonneberg
L&H	Leibe & Hofmann, Gera-Untermhaus
LHB	unknown
LL&S	Louis Lindner & Söhne, Sonneberg
L&M	unknown
LPL	Louis Philipp Luthardt, Neustadt
LS	Lambert & Samhammer, Sonneberg
LW&C	Louis Wolf & Co., Sonneberg/New York City

M

M	unknown
M	Ma.E. Maar, Mönchröden
MB	Arthur Schoenau, Sonneberg
MCo	Karl Müller & Co., Effelder
MKW	Josef Strasser, München
MMM	Ma.E. Maar, Mönchröden
MOA	Max Oscar Arnold, Neustadt
MR	Moritz Resek, Bohemia
MRW	Max Rudolph, Waltershausen
M&S	Müller & Straßburger, Sonneberg
MSS	Mylius Sperschneider, Sonneberg

N

NG	= Neugeborenes (=newborn), Geradhals (=straight neck),
	= Theodor Recknagel, Alexandrinenthal

Letter	Firm
NK	= **Neugeborenes** (=newborn), **Kurbelkopf** (=socket head),
	= Theodor Recknagel, Alexandrinenthal
NT	Nöckler & Tittel, Schneeberg
N&T	Nöckler & Tittel, Schneeberg

O

Letter	Firm
OB	Oskar Büchner, Ebersdorf
OCo	H. Offenbacher & Co. Nürnberg
OG	Otto Gans, Waltershausen
OIC	J.D. Kestner jr., Waltershausen
OS	Otto Schamberger, Sonneberg
OWN	Otto Wohlmann, Nürnberg

P

Letter	Firm
PH	Paul Hunaeus, Hannover
P&H	Pollak & Hoffmann, Bohemia
PM	Porzellanfabrik Mengersgereuth
PN	S. Bergmann jr. & Co./
	Porzellanfabrik Neuhaus
PR	Paul Rauschert, Pressig
PR	Hermann Rösel, Nürnberg
P&R	Plass & Roesner, Bohemia
PS	Paul Schmidt, Sonneberg
PSch	Peter Scherf, Sonneberg
PSSth	Paul Schmidt, Sonneberg
PZ	Paul Zierow, Berlin

R

Letter	Firm
R	Theodor Recknagel, Alexandrinenthal

Letter	Firm
RA	Theodor Recknagel, Alexandrinenthal
RB	Rempel & Breitung, Sonneberg
RBW	Richard Beck & Co., Waltershausen
RC	Robert Carl, Köppelsdorf
RDEP	Max Räder, Sonneberg
Rn	Porzellanfabrik Rauenstein
R&SS	Rauch & Schelhorn, Sonneberg
RBW	Richard Beck & Co., Waltershausen

S

S	Theodor Recknagel, Alexandrinenthal
S&C	Swaine & Co., Hüttensteinach (stamped)
S&C	Franz Schmidt & Co., Georgenthal
S&H	Simon & Halbig, Gräfenhain
SH	Simon & Halbig, Gräfenhain
SMB	Sigismund Markmann, Berlin
S&M	Seligman & Mayer, Sonneberg
SP	Sonneberger Porzellanfabrik, Sonneberg
SPBH	Schoenau & Hofmeister, Porzellanfabrik Burggrub
SPS	presumable Sonneberger Porzellanfabrik, Carl Müller, Sonneberg
SQ	Schützmeister & Quendt, Boilstädt
SS	M.F. Schelhorn, Sonneberg
SSN	S. Schwerin Nachf., Breslau
SUN	Sigmund Ullmann, Nürnberg
SUR	Seyfarth & Reinhardt, Waltershausen
SW	Strobel & Wilken, Sonneberg/New York City
S&W	Strobel & Wilken, Sonneberg/New York City
SWC	unknown

T

TH	Theodor Hörnlein, Sonneberg
TKB	M. Tersch, Berlin

Letter	Firm
TP	Theodor Pohl, Bohemia
TPI	Thüringer Puppenindustrie, Waltershausen
TPIW	Thüringer Puppenindustrie, Waltershausen
TR	unknown
TW	Theodor Wendt, Hamburg

V

VMB	Valentin Moritz Bruchlos, Eisfeld

W

W	Albert Wacker, Bayerische Celluloidwaren- fabrik, Nürnberg
W	Heubach, Kämpfe & Sontag, Wallendorf
W	E. Winkler, Sonneberg
W&Co	Wiefel & Co., Steinbach
WD	unknown
WEP	Wenzel Prouza, Bohemia
WG	F&W. Goebel, Oeslau
WK	Werner Krauth, Leipzig
WSK	Wiesenthal, Schindel & Kallenberg, Waltershausen
WKW	Strasser & Co., München
WP	Waltershäuser Puppenfabrik, Waltershausen
W&S	Walther & Sohn, Oeslau
WSt	Wilhelm Strunz, Nürnberg
WsT	Weiskirchlitzer Steingutfabrik, Bohemia
WuZI	Wagner & Zetsche, Ilmenau
WZ	Wagner & Zetsche, Ilmenau
WZI	Wagner & Zetsche, Ilmenau

Z

Z	Gottlieb Zinner & Söhne, Schalkau

The names and terms listed in the following are either
registered trademarks, or words used by porcelain
manufactories, doll factories or import houses.
They were found as marks or labels, or printed on the
packing. The registered terms of Rheinische Gummi- and
Celluloidfabrik of Mannheim-Neckarau (Turtle-mark) are not
considered here. This would go beyond the frame of this
publication, and will be the subject of another report
by the authors. However, the interested reader may find
the single terms in the frame of GM registrations under
Rheinische Gummi- and Celluloidfabrik. Comparing registered
trademarks with foreign doll literature may lead to some
misunderstandings. United States import houses had the same
trademarks registered as their own trademarks at different
points of time. The first registration had often been
made with the German authorities (or vice versa), thus two
different dates of registration could exist. The dates mentioned
in this publication refer exclusively to the year of
registration in Germany

Mark- or Article		Applied or used by the Firm
A		
ABC-Dolls	=	Butler Brothers, Sonneberg/New York City
Adeline	=	E. Liebermann, Neustadt
Adlon	=	O. Schamberger, Sonneberg
Admiral Dewey and his man	=	Cuno & Otto Dressel, Sonneberg
Agnes	=	Butler Brothers, Sonneberg/New York City
Aha-Puppe	=	Andreas Hofmann, Fürth
AHABE	=	Amberg & Hergershausen, Berlin
AI-AI	=	Arno Lützelberger, Ilmenau

Mark- or Article	=	Applied or used by the Firm
Alah	=	Anni Lonz, Koblenz
Albego	=	Alt, Beck & Gottschalck, Nauendorf
Alice	=	Porzellanfabrik Rauenstein
Alkico	=	A. Kiesewetter, Coburg
All Nation Comical	=	Cuno & Otto Dressel, Sonneberg
Alma	=	Armand Marseille, Köppelsdorf/ Geo. Borgfeldt & Co., Berlin/New York City
American Beauty	=	Robert Carl, Köppelsdorf
Americy Pet	=	F.M. Schilling, Sonneberg
American Queen	=	Otto Morgenroth, Sonneberg
Ameli	=	Kämmer & Reinhardt, Waltershausen
A mon Mignon	=	Fleischmann & Bloedel, Nürnberg
Amuso	=	A. Möller & Sohn, Georgenthal
Anna	=	Schwarzkopf & Fröber, Sonneberg
Apriko	=	Margarete Steiff, Giengen/ Albert Schlopsnies, München
ARI	=	A. Riedeler, Königsee
Arnola	=	Max Oscar Arnold, Neustadt
Arnoldia	=	Sing- und Sprechpuppen AG., Neustadt
Asador	=	Bauer & Richter, Stadtroda
Asta	=	Arthur Schoenau, Sonneberg
As You like	=	Buschow & Beck, Nossen
Autoliebchen	=	Arthur Schoenau, Sonneberg

B

Baby	=	Hermann Kröning, Gotha
Baby Bauz	=	Kämmer & Reinhardt, Waltershausen/ Käthe Kruse Werkstätten, Bad Kösen
Baby Belle	=	C.M. Bergmann, Waltershausen/ Geo. Borgfeldt & Co., Berlin/New York City

Mark- or Article	=	Applied or used by the Firm
Baby Betty	=	Armand Marseille, Köppelsdorf/
		Butler Brothers GmbH., Sonneberg
Baby Blanche	=	Simon & Halbig, Gräfenhain
Baby Bo-Kaye	=	Geo. Borgfeldt & Co., Berlin/New York City
Baby Bunting	=	Louis Lindner & Söhne, Sonneberg
Baby Bud	=	Butler Brothers, Sonneberg/New York City
Baby Cut	=	Heinrich Handwerck, Waltershausen
Baby Joan	=	Ernst Liebermann, Neustadt
Baby Gloria	=	Armand Marseille, Köppelsdorf
Baby Phyllis	=	Armand Marseille, Köppelsdorf
Baby Smiles	=	Geo. Borgfeldt & Co., Berlin/New York City
Baby Tufams	=	Louis Amberg & Son, Sonneberg/New York City
Bärbel-Puppe	=	Bärbel Wichmann, Berlin
Backfischpuppen	=	Cuno & Otto Dressel, Sonneberg
Baigneur habille	=	Wilhelm Simon & Co., Hildburghausen
Bambina	=	Cuno & Otto Dressel, Sonneberg
Beauty	=	Armand Marseille, Köppelsdorf/
		W.A. Cissna & Co., Chicago (USA)
Bebe Articule	=	Emil Pfeiffer, Vienna/
		F.E. Winkler, Sonneberg
Bebe Carmencita	=	Arthur Schoenau, Sonneberg
Bebe Coiffeure	=	Gutmann & Schiffnie, Sonneberg
Bebe Cosmopolite	=	Heinrich Handwerk, Waltershausen
Bebe Elite	=	Max Handwerck, Waltershausen
Bebe Habille	=	Carl Geyer, Sonneberg
Bebe l'Avenir	=	Gutmann & Schiffnie, Sonneberg/
		Gebr. Süssenguth, Neustadt
Bebe Kochniss	=	Carl Kochniss, Sonneberg
Bebe Princess	=	Gebr. Ohlhaver, Sonneber
Bebe Reclame	=	Heinrich Handwerck, Waltershausen
Bebe Superior	=	Heinrich Handwerck, Waltershausen
Bebe tout en bois	=	E. Dehler, Neustadt/
		Rudolf Schneider, Sonneberg

Mark- or Article	=	Applied or used by the Firm
Bebe Triomphe	=	Fleischmann & Bloedel, Nürnberg
Beha	=	Berthold Helk, Neustadt
Bella	=	Leo Nordschild, Berlin
Bellamit	=	A.M. Jochachimsczyk, Berlin
Bertha	=	Butler Brothers, Sonneberg/New York City
Bepi-Puppen	=	Bergische Puppenindustrie, Remscheid
Betsy	=	Geo. Borgfeld & Co., Berlin/New York City
Bette	=	J. D. Kestner jr., Waltershausen
Bi-Ba-Bo	=	Julius Jeidel, Frankfurt
Bi, Ba, Bo	=	Weise & Co., Leipzig
Biddy Baby	=	M. Kohnstamm & Co., Fürth
Billydoll	=	Margarete Steiff, Giengen
Bisculoid	=	Hertwig & Co., Katzhütte
Biskuit Imitation	=	A. Zeh, Sonneberg/
		Gebr. Haag, Sonneberg
Bisquitfacon	=	Barbara Schilling, Sonneberg
Bonnie Babe	=	Geo. Borgfeldt & Co., Berlin/New York City
Brüderchen	=	Friedrichsrodaer Puppenfabrik
Boy Scouts	=	Gutmann & Schiffnie, Sonneberg
Bubikopf	=	S. Plaut, Düsseldorf
Bufli	=	Resi Brandl, Berlin
Buporit	=	Baehr & Proeschild, Ohrdruf
Bussi	=	Willi Steiner, Freiburg/
		Eugen Knops, Freiburg
Butler	=	unknown
Butzi	=	J. Cyreck, München
Bye-Lo-Baby	=	Geo. Borgfeldt & Co., Berlin/New York City

C

Caho	=	Canzler & Hofmann, Sonneberg
Cama	=	Armand Marseille, Köppelsdorf
Campbell Kids	=	Josef Süßkind, Hamburg

Mark- or Article	=	Applied or used by the Firm
Campbell-Puppen	=	Otto Sauerteig, Neustadt
Caprice	=	Emil Bauersachs, Sonneberg
Carmencita	=	Arthur Schoenau, Sonneberg
Carl	=	Kämmer & Reinhardt, Waltershausen
Casadora	=	Huttinger & Buschor, Behringersdorf
Cebaso	=	Carl Beck & Alfred Schulze, Ohrdruf
Cecille	=	Martin Eichhorn, Sonneberg
Cefer	=	C.F. Reinhardt, Coburg
Cellulit	=	Kley & Hahn, Ohrdruf
Cellulobrin	=	Franz Schmidt & Co., Georgenthal
Cellunova	=	Kley & Hahn, Ohrdruf
Century Doll Co	=	J.D. Kestner jr., Waltershausen
Certa	=	Adolf Wislizenus, Waltershausen
Chantecler Doll	=	Geo. Borgfeldt & Co., Berlin/New York City/ Henze & Steinhäuser, Gehren/Leven & Sprenger, Sonneberg
Charakterpuppe	=	Kämmer & Reinhardt, Waltershausen
Charlie Carrot	=	Geo. Borgfeldt & Co., Berlin/New York City
Chondrogen	=	Max Räder, Sonneberg
Chubby	=	Louis Wolf & Co., Berlin/New York City
Cinderella Baby	=	C.M. Bergmann sen., Waltershausen
Cleo	=	Bayerische Celluloidwarenfabrik, Nürnberg
Columbia	=	Armand Marseille, Köppelsdorf/ C.M. Bergmann, Sonneberg/Carl Hart- mann, Neustadt/Geo. Borgfeldt & Co. Berlin/New York City
Com-A-Long	=	Geo. Borgfeldt & Co., Berlin/New York City
Coquette	=	Gebr. Heubach, Lichte
Cornoulioud-Doll	=	Max Handwerck, Waltershausen
Cupid	=	M. Kohnstamm & Co., Fürth
Cupido	=	Karl Standfuss, Deuben

D

DADA	=	Hermsdorfer Celluloidwarenfabrik
Daheim	=	Carl Hartmann, Neustadt
Dainty May	=	Demalcol, Catterfeld
Daisy	=	Geo. Borgfeldt & Co., Berlin/New York City/
		Edmond Ulrich Steiner, Sonneberg
DALABA	=	Arthur Schoenau, Sonneberg
Das deutsche Kind	=	Käthe Kruse Werkstätten, Bad Kösen
Darling	=	Strobel & Wilken, Sonneberg/New York City
Das kriechende Baby	=	Kley & Hahn, Ohrdruf
Das lachende Baby	=	Arthur Schoenau, Sonneberg
Das lebende Baby	=	Julius Henschel, Berlin
Das Neugeborene	=	Gustav Schmey, Sonneberg
Das strampelnde Baby	=	Kley & Hahn, Ohrdruf
Das süße Trudelchen	=	Johannes Kriege, Magdeburg
Das Riesenbaby	=	Kley & Hahn, Ohrdruf
Das Träumerchen	=	Käthe Kruse Werkstätten, Bad Kösen
Daumenlutscher	=	Richard Scherzer, Sonneberg/
(Suck-Thumb-Baby)		Carl Heumann, Sonneberg/Huttinger &
		Buschor, Behringersdorf
DEKAWE	=	Carl Herrmann, Potsdam/Deutsche
		Kolonial-Kapok-Werke AG., Berlin
Delly	=	Delly Puppenfabrik, Stuttgart
Der Bösewicht	=	Koenig & Wernicke, Waltershausen
Der deutsche Michel	=	Oscar Kirchner, Schalkau
Der heitere Fridolin	=	Fleischmann & Bloedel, Nürnberg
Der kleine Hansi	=	Wagner & Zetsche, Ilmenau
Der kleine Spatz	=	Bayerische Celluloidwarenfabrik,
		Nürnberg
Der kleine Mensch	=	Mittelland Gummiwerke, Hannover
Der rosige Liebling	=	Kämmer & Reinhardt, Waltershausen
Der Schelm	=	Kämmer & Reinhardt, Waltershausen

Mark- or Article	=	Applied or used by the Firm
Der Unart	=	Kämmer & Reinhardt, Waltershausen
Dewey, Admiral	=	Cuno & Otto Dressel, Sonneberg
Diana	=	Alfred Heller, Meiningen
Didi	=	Geo. Borgfeldt & Co., Berlin/New York City/
		Alt, Beck & Gottschalck, Nauendorf
Die kleine Hansi	=	Wagner & Zetsche, Ilmenau
Die kleine Range	=	Koenig & Wernicke, Walterhausen
Die Kokette	=	Kämmer & Reinhardt, Waltershausen
Die Potsdamer Soldaten	=	Käthe Kruse Werkstätten, Bad Kösen
Dollarprinzessin	=	Dr. Dora Petzold, Berlin
Dolly Dimple	=	Hamburger & Co., Berlin/New York City
		Butler Brothers, Sonneberg/New York City
Dolly Mine	=	Gans & Seyfarth, Waltershausen
Dolly Pat Travels	=	Richard Scherzer, Sonneberg
Dolly Varden	=	Cuno & Otto Dressel, Sonneberg/
		Butler Brothers, Sonneberg/New York City
Dora	=	Porzellanfabrik Rauenstein
Dorothy	=	Butler Brothers, Sonneberg/New York City
Dotty	=	Geo. Borgfeldt & Co., Berlin/New York City
Dreso-Puppe	=	Fritz Dressel, Sonneberg
Dry climate	=	Geo. Borgfeldt & Co., Berlin/New York City
Duchess	=	Armand Marseille, Köppelsdorf/
		Geo. Borgfeldt & Co., Berlin/New York City
Durabel	=	Kley & Hahn, Ohrdruf

E

EBASO	=	Emil Bauersachs, Sonneberg
ECCO	=	Eckstein & Co., Sonneberg
Eclaireur	=	Gutmann & Schiffnie, Nürnberg
Edelkind	=	Hugo Wiegand, Waltershausen
Eden Bebe	=	Fleischmann & Bloedel, Nürnberg

Mark- or Article	=	Applied or used by the Firm
Edith	=	Butler Brothers, Sonneberg/New York City
Einco	=	Eisenmann & Co., Fürth
Eleonore	=	Simon & Halbig, Gräfenhain/
		C.M. Bergmann, Sonneberg
Elfe	=	Gans & Seyfarth, Waltershausen
Elfenhaut	=	Amberg & Hergershausen, Berlin
Elfen-Puppe	=	Koenig & Wernicke, Waltershausen
Eli	=	Ernst Liebermann, Neustadt
Elie	=	Karl Müller & Co., Effelder
Elite	=	Max Handwerck, Waltershausen
ELLAR	=	Armand Marseille, Köppelsdorf
Elsa	=	unknown
Elsie	=	Geo. Borgfeldt & Co., Berlin/New York City
EMASO	=	Ma.E. Maar, Mönchröden
Erfordia	=	Otto Reipert, Erfurt
Erika	=	Simon & Halbig, Gräfenhain/
		Carl Hartmann, Neustadt
Esco	=	Sommer & Co., Berlin
Escora	=	Eduard Schmidt, Coburg
Esther	=	Butler Brothers, Sonneberg/New York City
Esy	=	E. Suchetzsky, Berlin
Ethel	=	Butler Brothers, Sonneberg/New York City
Excelsior	=	Louis Wolf & Co., Sonneberg/Heinrich
		Schmuckler, Liegnietz/J.D.Kestner jr.
		Waltershausen

F

Fahn	=	Reupke & Co., Sonneberg/
		F.A. Heubach Nachf., Sonneberg
Fancora-Wunderbaby	=	Franz Angermüller, Coburg
Fany	=	Armand Marseille, Köppelsdorf
Fanny	=	Armand Marseille, Köppelsdorf

Mark- or Article	=	Applied or used by the Firm
Fat Baby	=	J.D. Kestner jr., Waltershausen
Favorite Saxonia	=	Nöckler & Tittel, Schneeberg
Feldgrauen (=soldiers World War I)	=	Käthe Kruse Werkstätten, Bad Kösen/ Kley & Hahn, Ohrdruf/Margarete Steiff, Giengen
Fema	=	Beck & Co., Waltershausen
Fifth Ave Doll	=	Cuno & Otto Dressel, Sonneberg
Fingy-Legs-The-Tiny Tot	=	Geo. Borgfeldt & Co., Berlin/New York City
FLAGS OF ALL NATIONS	=	Cuno & Otto Dressel, Sonneberg
Flora	=	Eisfelder Puppenfabrik, Eisfeld
Florence	=	Butler Brothers, Sonneberg/New York City
Floresta	=	Scheyer & Co., Nürnberg
Florigotto	=	Florig & Otto, Dresden
Florodora	=	Armand Marseille, Köppelsdorf/ Geo. Borgfeldt & Co., Berlin/New York City
Flossie Fischer's Own Doll	=	Geo. Borgfeldt & Co., Berlin/New York City
Fluffy Ruffles	=	Max Schellhorn, Sonneberg
Friedel	=	E.W. Matthes, Berlin
Fridolin	=	Fleischmann & Bloedel, Nürnberg
Fritz	=	Emil Pfeiffer, Vienna
Frivona	=	F. Voigt Nachf., Sonneberg
Frizzi	=	John Heß, Hamburg

G

Gee Gee Dolly	=	E.J. Horsman C., New York
Gehrenia	=	Henze & Steinhäuser, Gehren
Geo	=	Gebr. Eckardt, Oberlind
Georgi	=	Eleonore Georgi, Koblenz
GESUE	=	Gebr. Süßenguth, Neustadt
GETE-Puppe	=	Gustav Thiele, Waltershausen

Mark- or Article	=	Applied or used by the Firm
Gibson Girl	=	Margarete Steiff, Giengen/
		J.D. Kestner jr., Waltershausen
Gladdie	=	Geo. Borgfeldt & Co., Berlin/New York City
Globe-Babies	=	Carl Hartmann, Neustadt
Gloriosa	=	J.D. Kestner jr., Waltershausen
Goldherz	=	Bruno Schmidt, Waltershausen
Goldstern	=	Adolf Hülss, Waltershausen
Granitol	=	Carl Hoffmeister, Sonneberg
Graziella Puppen	=	Max Sachs, Charlottenburg
Grecon-Puppe	=	Grete Cohn, Berlin
Gretchen	=	Adolf Wislizenus, Waltershausen
Grete	=	Kämmer & Reinhardt, Waltershausen/
		Porzellanfabrik Mengersgereuth
Gummoid	=	Nöckler & Tittel, Schneeberg
Guschi	=	Gutmann & Schiffnie, Sonneberg
Gymnastik Doll	=	Albin Heß, Schalkau

H

Habeka	=	Hermann von Berg, Köppelsdorf
Hafraco Puppe	=	Schöffl & Co., Berlin
Haliso	=	Heinrich Liebermann, Sonneberg
Hanco	=	Hahn & Co., Nürnberg
Handora	=	Ohrdrufer Handelsgesellschaft
Hanka	=	Gebr. Pfeiffer, Köppelsdorf
Hanna	=	Arthur Schoenau, Sonneberg
Hannelore	=	Hermann Pensky, Coburg
Hans	=	Kämmer & Reinhardt, Waltershausen
Hansa	=	Carl Hartmann, Neustadt
Hansa-Puppe	=	W. Reinick, Hamburg
Hänsel & Gretel	=	Moritz Pappe, Liegnitz
Hansi	=	Wagner & Zetsche, Ilmenau
Happifat	=	Geo. Borgfeldt & Co., Berlin/New York City

Mark- or Article	=	Applied or used by the Firm
Happy Hooligan	=	Geo. Borgfeldt & Co., Berlin/New York City
Hapusa	=	Hermann Hachmeister, Sonneberg
Harald	=	Wagner & Zetsche, Ilmenau
Haralit	=	Wagner & Zetsche, Ilmenau
Hawadit	=	Hammer Munitionswerk, Wallendorf
Heinerle	=	Helene Haeusler, Sonneberg
Hedi	=	S. Schwerin Nachf., Breslau
Heico	=	M. Heider & Co., Nürnberg
Heio-Beio	=	Scherzer & Fischer, Sonneberg
Heiterer Fridolin	=	Fleischmann & Bloedel, Nürnberg
Helen	=	unknown/Butler Brothers, Sonneberg/New York City
Helgünith	=	Oskar Günthel, Gräfenroda
Henny	=	Böhnke & Zimmermann, Königsberg
Henny Puppe	=	Loetel & Co., Braunschweig
Henza	=	Henze & Steinhäuser, Gehren
Herka	=	Martha Köllner, Ilmenau
Herkules	=	Josef Deuerlein, Nürnberg
Herz	=	Bruno Schmidt, Waltershausen
Herzi	=	Porzellanfabrik Mengersgereuth
Herzkäferchen	=	Bauer & Richter, Stadtroda
Herzlieb	=	Scherzer & Fischer, Sonneberg/
		Hugo Wiegand, Waltershausen
Herzpuppen	=	Herzpuppen-Fabrik, Berlin
Hesli	=	Heinrich Schmuckler, Liegnitz
Hewika	=	Hertwig & Co., Katzhütte
Hexe	=	unknown
Hilda	=	J.D. Kestner jr., Waltershausen
Hi-Way Henry	=	Geo. Borgfeldt & Co., Berlin/New York City
Hochtourist	=	Mathilde Sehm, Guben
Holzmasse	=	Cuno & Otto Dressel, Sonneberg/
		Julius Dorst, Sonneberg
Huberta	=	Emil Pfeiffer, Vienna
Hubsy-Puppen	=	Emil Pfeiffer, Vienna

Mark- or Article	=	Applied or used by the Firm

I

IGES	=	J.G. Escher & Sohn, Sonneberg
IGODI	=	Kohl & Wengenroth, Offenbach
Illco	=	Carl A. Illing & Co., Sonneberg
Imperial	=	Hamburger & Co., Sonneberg/New York City
Instructible Heads	=	Cuno & Otto Dressel, Sonneberg
Inge	=	Wagner & Zetsche, Ilmenau
Iris	=	Iris Beaumont, Berlin
Irvington	=	Geo. Borgfeldt & Co., Berlin/New York City
I-We-Em	=	Ines Wetzel, Berlin

J

Jackie Coogan	=	Harburger Gummiwaren-Fabrik/ Fleischmann & Bloedel, Nürnberg/ Gustav Förster, Neustadt
Japanese Baby	=	M. Kohnstamm & Co., Fürth
JDEN	=	Josef Deuerlein Nachf., Nürnberg
Jing-Go-Ring-Doll	=	Fritz Lutz, Sonneberg
Jointed Doll	=	Gans & Seyfarth, Waltershausen/ C.M. Bergmann, Waltershausen/ Adolf Wislizenus, Waltershausen
Jose	=	Johannes Sauerteig, Sonneberg
Jubilee Doll	=	Strobel & Wilken, Sonneberg/New York City
Juno	=	Karl Standfuss, Deuben
Just me	=	Armand Marseille, Köppelsdorf/ Geo. Borgfeldt & Co., Berlin/New York City
Jutta	=	Cuno & Otto Dressel, Sonneberg

K

Keep Smiling	=	Elise Israel, Zittau

Mark- or Article	=	Applied or used by the Firm
Kewpie	=	Hermann Voigt, Schaala/Carl Völker,
		Sonneberg/Karl Standfuss, Deuben/
		Geo. Borgfeldt & Co., Berlin/New York City/
		J.D. Kestner jr., Waltershausen
		Margarete Steiff, Giengen
Kid Doll	=	Carl Hoffmeister, Sonneberg
Kiddiejoy	=	Armand Marseille, Köppelsdorf
Kidolin	=	Carl Hoffmeister, Sonneberg
Kidlyne Doll	=	Carl Hoffmeister, Sonneberg
Kidette Doll	=	Carl Hoffmeister, Sonneberg
Kindertraum	=	Otto Gans, Waltershausen
Kissie	=	Cuno & Otto Dressel, Sonneberg
Klein Mammy	=	Kämmer & Reinhardt, Waltershausen
Kleiner Sonnenschein	=	Catterfelder Puppenfabrik
Knopf im Ohr	=	Margarete Steiff, Giengen
Königskinder	=	Koenig & Wernicke, Waltershausen
KO-KO	=	Geo. Borgfeldt & Co., Berlin/New York City
Kolundro	=	Martin Winterbauer, Nürnberg/Josef
		Deuerlein Nachf., Nürnberg/Kohler
		& Rosenwald, Nürnberg
Kowenko	=	Kohl & Wengenroth, Offenbach
Kronen Puppe	=	J.D. Kestner jr., Waltershausen
Künstlerkopf	=	Schoenau & Hoffmeister, Burggrub

L

La Belle	=	Heinrich Handwerck, Waltershausen
La Bonita	=	Heinrich Handwerck, Waltershausen
La Superba	=	Max Oscar Arnold, Neustadt
Lehowa	=	Lehowa, Sonneberg
Lieb Edelkind	=	Hugo Wiegand, Waltershausen
Liebling	=	Kämmer & Reinhardt, Waltershausen
lernt laufen		

Mark- or Article	=	Applied or used by the Firm
Liliput	=	Carl Geyer, Sonneberg (in USA registered by E.U. Steiner)
Lilly	=	Armand Marseille, Köppelsdorf
Linon	=	Isidor Eisenstaedt & Co., Waltershausen/Hermann Landshut & Co. Waltershausen
Lisa	=	Elise Israel, Zittau
Lithoid	=	Nöckler & Tittel, Schneeberg
Little Annie Rooney	=	Geo. Borgfeldt & Co., Berlin/New York City
Little Bright Eyes	=	Geo. Borgfeldt & Co., Berlin/New York City
Little sister	=	Geo. Borgfeldt & Co., Berlin/New York City
Little Snookums,the newlywed's Baby	=	Max Fr. Schellhorn, Sonneberg
Little Sunshine	=	Catterfelder Puppenfabrik/ Demalcol GmbH., Catterfeld
Little Sweetheart	=	Max Illfelder, Fürth
Lona-Künstlerpuppe	=	A. Schmidt, Dresden
Lopto	=	Thüringer Puppen- und Spielwaren- Export, Berlin
Lori	=	Swaine & Co., Hüttensteinach
Lotte	=	Victor Steiner, Sonneberg/ Cuno & Otto Dressel, Sonneberg
Lotti	=	Heinrich Handwerck, Waltershausen
Lucille	=	Martin Eichhorn, Sonneberg
Lullabye Baby	=	Martin Eichhorn, Sonneberg
Luta	=	Eg.M. Luthardt, Steinach
Lyro	=	Rolfes & Co., Berlin/ Franz Volpert, Charlottenburg

M

| Maba Künstlerpuppe | = | Max A. Barnikol, Sonneberg |

Mark- or Article	=	Applied or used by the Firm
Mabel	=	Armand Marseille, Köppelsdorf/ Butler Brothers, Sonneberg/New York City
Madame Butterfly	=	Max Handwerck, Waltershausen
Mafuka	=	Otto Scheyer & Co., Nürnberg
Majestic	=	Ernst Ulrich Steiner, Sonneberg/ Kley & Hahn, Ohrdruf/ Kämmer & Reinhardt, Waltershausen
Mamas Herzensschatz	=	Friedrichsrodaer Puppenfabrik
Mammy	=	Kämmer & Reinhardt, Waltershausen
Maquette	=	Pulvermacher & Westram, Sonneberg and Wilhelm Simon, Hildburghausen
Maria	=	Strasserpuppen-Werkstätten, Berlin
Marie	=	Kämmer & Reinhardt, Waltershausen
Margret	=	Armand Marseille, Köppelsdorf/ Cuno & Otto Dressel, Sonneberg
Marion	=	Butler Brothers, Sonneberg/New York City
Marta	=	Carl Hartmann, Neustadt
Marvel	=	J.D. Kestner jr., Waltershausen/ Butler Brothers, Sonneberg/New York City
Mausi	=	Robert Carl, Köppelsdorf
Maya	=	Geschw. Heinrich, Nürnberg
Max & Moritz	=	Kilian Cramer, Großbreitenbach/ Theodor Recknagel, Alexandrinenthal/ Margarete Steiff, Giengen/Mathilde Sehm, Guben/Kämmer & Reinhardt, Waltershausen/Kley & Hahn, Ohrdruf/ J.D. Kestner jr., Waltershausen
Maxi	=	Max Beuster, Kiel
May Blossom	=	Demalcol, Catterfeld/Alfred Lange, Friedrichsroda
McKinley	=	Cuno & Otto Dressel, Sonneberg
Mein Augenstern	=	Paul Zierow, Berlin
Mein Einziger	=	Kley & Hahn, Ohrdruf

Mark- or Article	=	Applied or used by the Firm
Mein Glückskind	=	Adolf Wislizenus, Waltershausen
Mein Goldherz	=	Bruno Schmidt, Waltershausen
Mein Goldstern	=	C.M. Bergmann, Waltershausen/ Adolf Hülß, Waltershausen
Mein Herz'l	=	Catterfelder Puppenfabrik
Mein Herzenskind	=	Wilhelm Buschow, Dresden
Mein kleiner Liebling	=	Kämmer & Reinhardt, Walterhausen
Mein kleiner Schlingel	=	Bauer & Richter, Stadtroda
Mein Kleines	=	Kämmer & Reinhardt, Waltershausen
Mein liebes Kind	=	Alfred Heller, Waltershausen
Mein Liebling	=	Kämmer & Reinhardt, Waltershausen
Mein Lieblingsbaby	=	Kämmer & Reinhardt, Waltershausen
Mein Nesthäckchen	=	Adolf Hülß, Waltershausen
Mein neuer Liebling	=	Kämmer & Reinhardt, Waltershausen
Mein rosiger Liebling	=	Kämmer & Reinhardt, Waltershausen
Mein Sonnenschein	=	Catterfelder Puppenfabrik
Mein Stern	=	Henriette Dunker, Hamburg
Mein Stolz	=	Koenig & Wernicke, Waltershausen
Mein süßer Liebling	=	Kämmer & Reinhardt, Waltershausen
Mein süßer Schlingel	=	Rodaer Puppenfabrik Bauer & Richter
Mein Wunschkind	=	Arthur Schoenau, Sonneberg
Mein Ziergold	=	Elisabeth Schwarz, Gotha
Meine Einzige	=	Kley & Hahn, Ohrdruf
Meine Goldperle	=	Alfred Heller, Waltershausen
Meine Goldsternchen	=	Bruno Schmidt, Waltershausen
Melitta	=	Edmund Edelmann, Sonneberg
Merry Widow	=	Max Illfelder, Fürth
Mew Puss	=	Johann Heinrich Kletzin & Co., Coburg
Mi Encanto	=	Seligmann & Mayer, Sonneberg
Mia	=	M. Hecht, Nietleben

173

Mark- or Article	=	Applied or used by the Firm
Miblu	=	Kämmer & Reinhardt, Waltershausen/ Rheinische Gummi- und Celluloid, Fabrik, Mannheim/Koenig & Wernicke, Waltershausen
Michel	=	A. Michaelis, Rauenstein
Michu	=	Fleischmann & Blodel, Nürnberg
Miles	=	Cuno & Otto Dressel, Sonneberg
Mimi	=	Geo. Borgfeldt & Co., Berlin/New York City/ Alt, Beck & Gottschalck, Nauendorf
Mimosa	=	Mimosa, Ochenbruck bei Nürnberg
Mine	=	Edmund Edelmann, Sonneberg
Minverva	=	Buschow & Beck, Nossen
Minnie Spinach	=	Geo. Borgfeldt & Co., Berlin/New York City
Miss Elisabeth	=	Zum Puppenheim, Sonneberg
Miss Millionaire	=	Butler Brothers, Sonneberg/New York City
Miss Royal	=	Zum Puppenheim, Sonneberg
Mit dem Goldreif	=	Ilse Müller, Berlin
MOA	=	Max Oscar Arnold, Neustadt
Mobi	=	Hermann Schiemer, Nürnberg
Moko	=	M. Kohnstamm & Co., Fürth
Mona	=	Edmund Edelmann, Sonneberg
Mona Lisa	=	Gutmann & Schiffnie, Sonneberg
Mon Petit Coeur	=	Bruno Schmidt, Waltershausen
Monte-Carlo-Genre	=	Galluba & Hofmann, Ilmenau
Monty	=	Jos. Süsskind, Hamburg
Mosca	=	Max Mocsardini & Co., Berlin
Mothers Darling	=	M. Kohnstamm & Co., Fürth
MÖKA	=	Müller & Kaltwasser, Rauenstein
Muing	=	W. Goebel, Sonneberg
Muk	=	Elise Israel, Zittau
Muschi	=	Martha Lehmann, Dresden
Mutzipuppe	=	Ch. Kirchoff, Berlin
My Annemarie	=	Wilhelm Follender, Düsseldorf

Mark- or Article	=	Applied or used by the Firm
My Cherub	=	Arthur Schoenau, Sonneberg
My Companion	=	Armand Marseille, Köppelsdorf/
		Louis Wolf & Co., Sonneberg/New York City
My Darling	=	Kämmer & Reinhardt, Waltershausen
My Dearie	= ʼ	Otto Gans, Waltershausen and Wiesenthal,
		Schindel & Kallenberg, Waltershausen for
		Geo. Borgfeldt & Co., New York
My Dream Baby	=	Armand Marseille, Köppelsdorf/
		Arranbee Doll & Co., New York
My Darling	=	Kämmer & Reinhardt, Waltershausen
My Fairy	=	Seyfarth & Reinhardt, Waltershausen
My Girlie	=	Geo. Borgfeldt & Co., Berlin/New York City
My Honey	=	Eduard Römhild, Sonneberg
My Honey-Dolls	=	Nordicus Colonda Werke, Sonneberg
My little Darling	=	Hermann Kröning, Gotha
My Pearl	=	Hermann Steiner, Sonneberg
My Pet	=	Buschow & Beck, Nossen
My Playmate	=	Armand Marseille, Köppelsdorf/
		Geo. Borgfeldt & Co., Berlin/New York City/
		Koenig & Wernicke, Waltershausen
My Sweetheart	=	B. Illfelder & Co., Fürth/
		Adolf Wislizenus, Waltershausen
My Queen Doll	=	Gebr. Ohlhaver, Sonneberg

N

Nanette	=	M. Kohnstamm & Co., Fürth
Natura	=	P. Hunaeus, Hannover
Naughty	=	Kämmer & Reinhardt, Waltershausen
Nesthäkchen	=	Adolf Hülß, Waltershausen
New Born Babe	=	Louis Amberg & Son, Sonneberg/New York City
Niddy Impekoven	=	Selma von Hasberg, Frankfurt

Mark- or Article	=	Applied or used by the Firm
Nobbikid	=	Armand Marseille, Köppelsdorf/
		Geo. Borgfeldt & Co., Berlin/New York City
Nobrake	=	Vereinigte Spielwarenfabriken,
		Waltershausen/Schmidt & Goerke,
		Waltershausen
Nollipolli	=	Kämmer & Reinhardt, Waltershausen
Nora	=	Nora Puppenfabrik, Sonneberg
Noris	=	Carl Debes & Sohn, Hof
Nöris	=	Bayerische Celluloidwarenfabrik, Nürnberg
Norma	=	Porzellanfabrik Limbach

O

Oco	=	Offenbach & Co., Nürnberg
Oga	=	Otto Gans, Waltershausen
Old Glory	=	Adolf Wislizenus, Waltershaus
Old Rip	=	unknown
Olympia	=	unknown
Ormond	=	D.H. Wagner & Sohn, Grünhainichen
Our Baby	=	Louis Wolf & Co., Sonneberg
Our Fairy	=	Louis Wolf & Co., Sonneberg
Our Pet	=	Gebr. Eckardt, Oberlind/
		Armand Marseille, Köppelsdorf

P

Paddy Potato	=	Geo. Borgfeldt & Co., Berlin/New York City
Paladin Babies	=	Carl Hartmann, Neustadt/
		Kämmer & Reinhardt, Waltershausen
Pansy	=	Geo. Borgfeldt & Co., Berlin/New York City
PAMA-Stimmen	=	G. Herold, Neustadt
Panta	=	Kämmer & Reinhardt, Waltershausen
Patent-Head	=	Fritz Vogel, Sonneberg

Mark- or Article	=	Applied or used by the Firm
Patent-Lederbebe	=	presumable Wagner & Zetsche, Ilmenau
Patentmasse	=	L.R. Hörchner & Co., Friedrichsrode/
		Kämmer & Reinhardt, Waltershausen
Papp-Head	=	Simon Junghans, Rittersgrün
Pat-a-cake	=	A. Luge & Co., Sonneberg
Peha	=	P. Hunaeus, Hannover
Pehaco	=	Hermann Pensky, Coburg
Perfectolid	=	Arthur Schoenau, Sonneberg
Perlico-Perlaco	=	Fleischmann & Bloedel, Nürnberg
PESO	=	Paul Schmidt, Sonneberg
Pet Names	=	Butler Brothers, Sonneberg/New York City
Peter	=	Kämmer & Reinhardt, Waltershausen
Peter Pan Playtoys	=	M.Fr. Schellhorn, Sonneberg
Phyllis Doll	=	Schmidt & Nüchter, Gröfenroda
Phoenix	=	Harburger Gummiwaren-Fabrik
PIGO	=	Puppenindustrie Gotha
Pioneer	=	Carl Hartmann, Neustadt
Pipa	=	D.H. Wagner & Sohn, Grünhainichen
Pirola	=	D.H. Wagner & Sohn, Grünhainichen
Pirouette	=	D.H. Wagner & Sohn, Grünhainichen
Pfiffikus	=	Koenig & Wernicke, Waltershausen/
		Franz Kiesewetter, Neustadt
Playmate	=	Emil Bauersachs, Sonneberg
Plombe in der Hand	=	Rudolf Säuberlich, Berlin
Pola Puppen	=	Thüringer Puppenindustrie, Gotha
Polait	=	M. Polack, Waltershausen
Poppy Dolls	=	Cuno & Otto Dressel, Sonneberg
Porzellanit	=	Kämmer & Reinhardt, Waltershausen
Potsdamer Soldaten	=	Käthe Kruse Werkstätten, Bad Kösen
Pauline	=	Butler Brothers, Sonneberg/New York City
Powerful Katrinka	=	Geo. Borgfeldt & Co., Berlin/New York City
Primrose	=	Waltershäuser Puppenfabrik
Primula	=	Thüringer Puppen- & Spielwaren-Export, Berlin

Mark- or Article	=	Applied or used by the Firm
Princess	=	Armand Marseille, Köppelsdorf/
		Kley & Hahn, Ohrdruf/Geo. Borgfeldt
		& Co., Berlin/New York City
Princess Elizabeth	=	Arthur Schoenau, Sonneberg/
		Christian Hopf, Neustadt
Prinzess Bett	=	M. Kohnstamm & Co., Fürth
Prinzess Sibylla	=	Hermann Eckstein, Neustadt
Prinzess Wunderhold	=	Arthur Schoenau, Sonneberg
Prize Baby	=	Geo. Borgfeldt & Co., Berlin/New York City
Puck	=	Florig & Otto, Dresden
Puppe der Zukunft	=	Gebr. Süssenguth, Neustadt
(=Doll of the Future)	=	H. Wordtmann, Hamburg
Puspi		

Q

| Queen Louise | = | Armand Marseille, Köppelsdorf |
| Queen Quality | = | Adolf Wislizenus, Waltershausen |

R

Racker	=	Gans & Seyfarth, Waltershausen
rar/use	=	Adolf Wislizenus, Waltershausen
Reformpuppe	=	Georg Becker, Hagen
Reg'lar Fellars	=	Geo. Borgfeldt & Co., Berlin/New York City
Reso	=	Schilling & Zitzmann, Sonneberg
Revalo	=	Carl Harmus jr., Sonneberg/
		Gebr. Ohlhaver, Sonneberg/ Ernst
		Heubach, Köppelsdorf
Rinaldo	=	Berthold Helk, Neustadt
Rita	=	Porzellanfabrik Limbach
Rock-A-Bye-Baby	=	Cuno & Otto Dressel, Sonneberg
Roli Cellowachs	=	Kämmer & Reinhardt, Waltershausen
Rollschuhläufer	=	Bernhnard Zehner, Schalkau

Mark- or Article	=	Applied or used by the Firm
Roma	=	Plass & Roessner, Bohemia
Roscamp-Puppen-Fantasien	=	Katarina Roscamp, Berlin
Roschco	=	Robert Schneider, Coburg
Rosebud	=	Armand Marseille, Köppelsdorf/ M. Illfelder & Co., Fürth
Rose-Puppe	=	F. Welsch, Berlin
Rosi	=	Kämmer & Reinhardt, Waltershausen
Rotkäppchen	=	Rotkäppchen GmbH., Berlin/ 0. Ludwig, Gehren
Royal	=	J.D. Kestner jr., Waltershausen
Ruth	=	Butler Brothers, Sonneberg/New York City
Ruthea-Puppen	=	Grete Ruhl, Leipzig

S

Sag'Schnucki zu mir	=	Wally Fischel, Berlin
Sam Boy	=	M. Kohnstamm & Co., Fürth
Sampson	=	Cuno & Otto Dressel, Sonneberg
Santa	=	Simon & Halbig, Gräfenhain/ Hamburger & Co., Berlin/New York City
Schalk	=	Gans & Seyfarth, Waltershausen
Schelmaugen	=	Kämmer & Reinhardt, Waltershausen
Schieler	=	August Friedrich Carl, Sonneberg
Schlenkerchen	=	Käthe Kruse Werkstätten, Bad Kösen
Schneeflöckchen	=	Nöckler & Tittel, Schneeberg
Schneeglöckchen	=	Nöckler & Tittel, Schneeberg
Schneewittchen	=	Kley & Hahn, Ohrdruf
Schwesterchen	=	Friedrichsrodaer Puppenfabrik
Seco	=	Strauss-Eckardt C., Inc. New York/ Gebr. Eckardt, Oberlind
Shirley Temple	=	Armand Marseille, Köppelsdorf
Sico	=	Eduard Schmidt, Coburg

Mark- or Article	=	Applied or used by the Firm
Sicora	=	Löffler & Dill, Sonneberg/ Eduard Schmidt, Coburg
Siegfried	=	J.D. Kestner jr., Waltershausen
Siha	=	Simon Hahn, Zirndorf
Snookums	=	Max Friedrich Schellhorn, Sonneberg
Sonnenpuppe	=	Welsch & Co., Sonneberg
Sonny Boy	=	Hugo Wiegand, Waltershausen
South Sea Baby	=	A. Luge & Co., Sonneberg
Special	=	Adolf Wislizenus, Waltershausen/ /Kley & Hahn, Ohrdruf
Spezial	=	C.M. Bergmann, Waltershausen/ F. Kuhles, Catterfeld
Stabil	=	Robert Richter, Waltershausen/ Emil Heyer & Co., Gräfenroda
Star	=	H. Eckstein, Neustadt
Stella	=	J. Stellmacher, Steinheid
Storch	=	Schwäbische Celluloidwarenfabrik, Mengen
Strampelchen	=	Edith Maus, Braunschweig
Strandfee	=	O. Eberwein & Co., Hamburg
Südsee-Baby	=	A. Luge & Co., Sonneberg
Suck Thumb Baby	=	Carl Heumann, Sonneberg
Sugar Plum	=	Geo. Borgfeldt, & Co., Berlin
SUN	=	Sigmund Ullmann, Nürnberg
Superba	=	unknown
Superior	=	Georg Lutz, Sonneberg/Cuno & Otto Dressel, Sonneberg/Müller & Strasburger, Sonneberg/Fleischmann & Co., Sonneberg/Heinrich Handwerck, Waltershausen
SUR	=	Seyfarth & Reinhardt, Waltershausen
Susie	=	Cuno & Otto Dressel, Sonneberg
Susi-Künstlerpuppen	=	Susi Künstlerpuppen, Stuttgart
Sweet Nell	=	Hugo Wiegand, Waltershausen
Syco	=	Sieder & Co., Plauen

Mark- or Article	=	Applied or used by the Firm

T

Taft	=	unknown
Tago	=	P. Bühl & Tannewitz, Gotha
Tausendschönchen	=	Franz Schmidt & Co., Georgenthal
Tebu	=	Theodor Buschbaum, Wallendorf
Teenie Weenie	=	Geo. Borgfeldt & Co., Berlin/New York City
Tessie	=	M. Kohnstamm & Co., Fürth
The Base Ball Fan	=	Max Friedrich Schellhorn, Sonneberg
The Dollar Princess	=	Kley & Hahn, Ohrdruf
The Duchess Dressed Doll	=	M. Kohnstamm & Co., Fürth
The Fairy Kid	=	Peter Scherf, Sonneberg
The Favorite Doll	=	Kämmer & Reinhardt, Waltershausen for F.A.O. Schwarz, New York
The Flirt	=	Kämmer & Reinhardt, Waltershausen
The Handwercks Celebrated Doll	=	Max Handwerck, Waltershausen
The International Doll	=	Geo. Borgfeldt & Co., Berlin/New York City
The Jolly Jester	=	Geo. Borgfeldt & Co., Berlin/New York City
The Skipper	=	Geo. Borgfeldt & Co., Berlin/New York City
The Sonny Boy	=	M. Kohnstamm & Co., Fürth
Thuringia	=	Carl Hartmann, Neustadt/ Porzellanfabrik Thuringia/ A. Luge & Co., Sonneberg/Thuringia AG., Hamburg
Thürpuin	=	Thüringer Puppen Industrie, Waltershausen
Tiny Tots	=	Geo. Borgfeldt & Co., Berlin/New York City
Tipple Topple	=	Emil Pfeiffer, Vienna
Tommy Turnip	=	Geo. Borgfeldt & Co., Berlin/New York City
Tootsie	=	Geog Borgfeldt & Co., Berlin/New York City
Torino	=	Berthold Helk, Neustadt
Tout Bois-All Wood	=	F.M. Schilling, Sonneberg

Mark- or Article	=	Applied or used by the Firm
Trebor	=	Porzellanfabrik Mengersgereuth
Triumph Bebe	=	Max Handwerck, Waltershausen
Trutzi	=	Johannes Rejall, Dresden

U

Ulla Puppe	=	Arthur Gotthelf, Remscheid
Unbreakable	=	Lambert & Samhammer, Sonneberg
Undine	=	(see Mechanicle Dolls)
Unerreicht	=	Adolph Harras Nachf., Großbreitenbach
Universal-Puppe	=	Carl Bergner, Sonneberg
Uncle Sam	=	Cuno & Otto Dressel, Sonneberg
Unsere goldigen Drei	=	Gebr. Heubach, Lichte
Unsere kleine Mammy	=	Kämmer & Reinhardt, Waltershausen
Unsere süßen Mädel	=	Gebr. Heubach, Lichte
Ursula	=	E.W. Matthes, Berlin
Unbreakable	=	Lambert & Samhammer, Sonneberg
Uwanta	=	Geo. Borgfeldt & Co., Berlin/New York City

V

Vanta Baby	=	Louis Amberg & Son, Sonneberg/New York City
Victoria Jointed Doll	=	W.Fr. Schönhut, Hermannstadt
Viktoria	=	Julius Hering, Köppelsdorf/ Cuno & Otto Dressel, Sonneberg/ Heinrich Schmuckler, Liegnitz
Viktoriababies	=	G. Gebert, Berlin
Viktoria Luise	=	Carl Hartmann, Neustadt
Viola	=	Hamburger & Co., Berlin/ Schoenau & Hoffmeister, Burggrub
Violet	=	Ernst Liebermann, Neustadt
Virginia Ginny for short	=	Geo. Borgfeldt & Co., Berlin/New York City
Vivi	=	A. Gorrigenes & Co., Berlin/ Geo. Borgfeldt & Co., Berlin/New York City

Mark- or Article	=	Applied or used by the Firm
Vöglein	=	Emma Vogel, Berlin

W

Waldkind	=	Vereinigung Finsterberger Puppenmacher
Walküre	=	Kley & Hahn, Ohrdruf
Wally	=	Porzellanfabrik Limbach
Walpu	=	Waltershäuser Puppenfabrik, Waltershausen
Walter	=	Kämmer & Reinhardt, Waltershausen
Waschecht	=	Cuno & Otto Dressel, Sonneberg/ Kämmer & Reinhardt, Waltershauen/ F.M. Schilling, Sonneberg
Washable Doll	=	Cuno & Otto Dressel, Sonneberg/ Kämmer & Reinhardt, Waltershausen/ F.M. Schilling, Sonneberg
WEEGEM	=	W.G. Müller, Sonneberg
Weimarpüppchen	=	Thüringer Stoffpuppen-Fabrik, Bad Berka
Weinende (=crying)	=	Albert Schachne, Nürnberg/ Hertel, Schwab & Co., Stutzhausen
Whistling Jim	=	Gebr. Heubach, Lichte
Wide Awake	=	Butler Brothers, Sonneberg/New York City
Wildfang	=	Wagner & Zetsche, Ilmenau
Wimpern ges.gesch.	=	Simon & Halbig, Gräfenhain/ Heinrich Handwerck, Waltershausen
Wunderkind	=	J.D. Kestner jr., Waltershausen

X

xtra	=	Geo. Borgfeldt & Co., Berlin/New York City